HENNING HAI LEE YANG can trace his family tree back over a thousand years to Yang Chiun Pun, one of China's most famous fortune-tellers. Although Henning Hai Lee Yang was educated as a business economist and a marine engineer, he has followed in his illustrious forefather's footsteps by devoting himself to a highly successful career in Chinese fortune-telling. He specializes in *Mian Xiang* (the Chinese art of face reading), Chinese astrology and *feng shui*. Based in Oslo, he is frequently asked to appear on radio and television programmes the world over, and is a regular contributor to newspapers and magazines. He is the author of a popular series of annual Chinese horoscope books, also published by Vega.

by the same author

The Year of the Dragon

Chinese Horoscopes for 2001: The Year of the Snake

forthcoming

Chinese Horoscopes for 2002: The Year of the Horse

Mian Xiang

The Chinese Art of Face Reading

Henning Hai Lee Yang

vega

A catalogue record for this book is
available from the British Library.

ISBN 1-84333-020-2
Printed in Great Britain by
Creative Print and Design (Wales)

© Vega 2001

A member of the Chrysalis Group plc

Published in 2001 by
Vega
8-10 Blenheim Court
Brewery Road
London N7 9NY

Visit our website at
www.chrysalisbooks.co.uk

CONTENTS

3. The Upper Part of the Face

The Ears

The Forehead

The Eyebrows

The Eyes

4. The Middle Part of the Face

The Nose

The Philtrums

The Cheekbones

5. The Lower Part of the Face

The Mouth

The Teeth

Laughter Lines

The Chin

6. Personal Appearance

The Hair

The Skin

The Forehead Aura

7. Mastering the Physical Languages

Introduction

What is *Mian Xiang*?

NOTHING IS MORE INFORMATIVE than the human face, if you know how to read it. The ancient Chinese art of *Mian Xiang*, or face reading, explains how to read a person's character and fortunes through his or her physical appearance. It is akin to the Western study of physiognomy but far more ancient. In *Mian Xiang*, each feature of the face is thought of as an individual building block and is carefully studied; then the separate interpretations are combined to arrive at a comprehensive conclusion about the fate of the face's owner.

Analysing a person is really rather easy if you know how to interpret the different features. It is as if the person were made of glass: what is on the inside – their character and luck in life – seems to be shown in their outer aspect. To a certain degree, this much is already obvious to most of us: if we are happy and satisfied, our outer aspect will reveal this automatically. If we are sad, our face and body language will disclose this too. Likewise, we can tell that a person with smooth skin, whose face is in proportion and has no wrinkles or scars, is probably someone who has never experienced any difficulties in life. By contrast, a lot of wrinkles or scars will automatically reveal someone who has endured great struggles and has fought to get by in life.

However, at times the glass surrounding a person's inner character can seem too thick, and in such instances it can be difficult to look straight into that person's core. But those who are trained in face reading and can understand the different features will be able to tell a lot about that person nevertheless, such as whether he or she is a good-hearted or difficult individual.

In *Mian Xiang*, it is said that the face changes in accordance with the mind and heart. It is thus quite natural that our faces should undergo many changes as we age. Everything in this world is subject to change, and our faces cannot escape this iron rule. (See chapter 2 for more information about age mapping.) Our faces reflect our prospects in many different ways: good deeds and noble intentions will bring about positive changes to our destinies that are also reflected in our faces, while bad deeds and malicious intentions will cause unfortunate changes. This golden rule of face reading should be rather encouraging for those not blessed by good fortune or a particularly pleasing face at birth, as they may be able to improve their prospects as well as their looks through their actions. If, on the other hand, you have been born with a naturally pleasing face and a seemingly happy destiny, you too should bear this principle in mind, for nothing is constant, least of all good fortune.

As our faces reflect both our prospects and our characters, the ability to read faces can unlock the secrets of both the present and the future. It can even be applied to our appreciation of the past. The relevance and scope of *Mian Xiang* becomes even clearer from a brief consideration of its history.

The History of Chinese Face Reading

The Chinese art of *Mian Xiang*, or face reading, dates back many thousands of years. It would, however, be wrong to believe that it derives from the *I Ching*, the earliest and best-known Chinese book on divination, although this work profoundly influenced the general development of Chinese culture. Instead, *Mian Xiang* was developed over many years through the gathering of information and statistical findings.

There were schools that taught face-reading skills as early as 403–221 BC, in the period of the Warring States; some say they existed as early as 481 BC. Probably the most famous of these schools was the one taught by Gui Gu Tze (475–403 BC), the Master of the Devil Gorge, who was not only an expert in face reading, but also a master of military strategy. Gui Gu Tze's most famous students were Pang Juan and Sun Bin. Sun Bin is widely believed to be the author of the world-famous tract *The Art of War* (although my own research suggests that this is not the case). Sun Bin took office as an advisor to the prime minister in the state of Qi, while Pang Juan became the commander-in-chief of the state of Wei. They were two of Gui Gu Tze's best students, but, instead of remaining friends, they became deadly enemies.

Cho Kuo Liang (*c.* AD 181–234) is yet another famous face-reading character in Chinese political history. In about AD 207, he helped Liu Bei, the descendant of the Han dynasty, to obtain power in Western China and to establish the Shu kingdom in that region. He held office as the prime minister of Shu, and was also a famous general and astrologer. He knew how to pick the right man for the right office, and it is said that he combined his great wisdom with his clairvoyant skills to defeat his enemies. His loyalty, tactical skill and insight were famous throughout China, and even today many Chinese people worship him as a saint for his righteousness and wisdom. He also wrote several books about the art of *Mian Xiang*.

In the period of transition between Tsui dynasty and the Tang dynasty (*c.* AD 700), one of my forefathers, Yang Chiu Pun (c. AD 581–688), is known to have practised *feng shui* and face reading. His family name 'Yang' means 'the Willow Tree', and Chiu Pun means 'helping the poor'. He gained a reputation as a tutor and a sort of saviour. China was going through a very turbulent period at this time and was locked in civil war.

There are many interesting legends concerning the face-reading talents of Li Shen Feng (AD 589–686), who was also involved with the protagonists of the civil war. One story tells how Li Shen Feng was invited to the home of Li Yuan, who was a powerful general stationed in the capital city of the Shanxi province in Northern China. Having made some very interesting observations about the general, Li Shen Feng turned to gaze at the general's second son, Li Shi Min, who was only thirteen years old. Li Shen Feng told the general that the face of his son combined the features of a dragon with those of a phoenix. This indicated that Li Shi Min would become Emperor of China and that he would save the country from anarchy at the age of twenty. Sure enough, when Li Shi Min turned twenty, he led a victorious army that conquered the whole country. After killing his older brother Li Qian Cheng and younger brother Li Yuan Qi, Li Shi Min succeeded to the throne in AD 626 and named his empire the Tang Dynasty.

After Li Shi Min became emperor, Li Shen Feng was offered a post at the Tang court and was asked by the emperor to continue to foretell the future of the empire. He was invited to the palace on many occasions. On one visit, Li was particularly impressed by one among the hundreds of concubines that he met, declaring that she had 'a pair of dragon eyes and a neck of a phoenix'. He wrote in his annals that one day this concubine, Wu Ze Tian, would be the head of the country. Once again, his prediction was accurate: in AD 690 Wu Ze Tian became the first empress to have complete power in China.

Yuan Tian Gang (AD 598–669) was another famous face reader of the early Tang dynasty. He came from Chengdu in the province of Szequan, and was famous for his ability to predict the fortunes of the entire nation as well as those of individuals. Yuan was the author of *Pictures of Pushing on Your Back* (AD 649), which remained a forbidden book for many centuries. It contains predictions written mostly in puns, which can only be decoded with great skill. Usually the meanings only become clear once the historical events alluded to have occurred. We Chinese think of this book in much the same way as Westerners regard the writings of Nostradamus.

Even in recent times, Chinese leaders have been interested in the art of face reading. Chiang Kai-shek (1887–1975) frequently used face analysis to help him find the right general for particular military manoeuvres. Before the major military showdown known as the 'Huai Hai Campaign' (1948) in the civil war between Chiang Kai-shek and Mao Tse Tung, Chiang spent many sleepless nights trying to find a suitable commander-in-chief for his army. He hoped that the individual fortunes of his key generals would help to determine the outcome of the war and bring good luck to his regime. At last, he decided that Liu Zhi, a well-known but mediocre general, should be the one to lead his forces. This unusual choice surprised everyone and, unfortunately for Chiang, his decision was not completely vindicated: the Huai Hai Campaign turned out to be his 'Waterloo'. From then on, the army was forced into all-out defence and collapsed rapidly. However, curiously enough, Liu Zhi was the only one of the top six generals on the nationalist side to return safely. The other five either committed suicide or were killed in action or captured. Following the defeat and ensuing flight of Chiang Kai-shek and his followers to the island of Taiwan in 1949, face reading, hand reading and the *I Ching* were all banned in China for about four decades. Mao Tse Tung regarded religion as poison and all Chinese fortune-telling techniques as 'feudal superstition'. However, because he was born in the year of the Snake, Mao often spoke with two tongues: although he publicly forbade the Chinese to believe or practise fortune-telling, he was privately a firm believer in the art.

In modern China, the government has tended to turn a blind eye to the whole business of fortune-telling, so the art of face reading has flourished. One proof of its growing popularity is that more and more Chinese companies are hiring fortune-tellers to read the faces of their employees. One Shanghai-based face reader in particular has been enjoying excellent business for years, ever since he predicted that Chiang Ze Ming would come to power after Deng Xiaoping in the wake of the government crackdown on the student movement in Tiananmen Square in 1989. There is no doubt that the fascinating art of face reading will continue to play a significant role in political, social, cultural and personal events in China and other countries that are influenced by the Chinese way of thinking.

The technique of face reading has been refined through the ages, but the fundamental principles have remained more or less unchanged since the days of ancient China. However, it is clear that our modern society is quite different to those of the past. For instance, equal education and the women's liberation movement have created unprecedented opportunities for women. These days, there is hardly anything that men can accomplish that lies beyond the reach of women. This book reflects these changes: over approximately thirty years of study, I have made certain modifications to the art to reflect the lives of men and women today, and to show how the basic principles of *Mian Xiang* apply to the faces of Westerners as well as to those of Orientals.

Face Reading and the
Different Human Races

Recent scientific research shows that our faces are a bit like computers that have been biologically programmed to show certain expressions, such as whether we are joyful, surprised, sad, afraid or disgusted. Identical ways of expressing pleasure, fear, surprise, anger and interest are seen all over the world: these are described in chapter 7. These universal expressions can be understood regardless of language differences or national boundaries: there is no need for words.

When it comes to reading emotions, women are usually much more capable than men. Men, for example, may read happiness in a woman's face quite easily, but a woman has to be very sad before most men get the message. Nonetheless, in many respects our faces are the most personal communication tools that we have at our disposal, regardless of how skilled other people are at interpreting them.

I have done careful research into the different human races, and have come to the conclusion that the fundamental principles of face reading apply to all of them without exception. When I analyse Chinese faces, I cannot find any major differences between them and those of the other races. It is true that many Chinese people have very broad noses, which is a sign of commercial acumen, a quality that is something of a national characteristic. However, a big nose denotes that its owner is ambitious and self-assured, whether it appears on a Chinese or an African person, and you can find people with small noses (a sign of timidity) in every race. A high nose is an indication of idealism, and is found on people who are leaders or who have leadership qualities, whatever their race.

The Many Benefits of Face Reading

If you master the art of face reading, you will be able to use your skills wherever you are and whomever you encounter. As well as analysing the faces and fortunes of friends and family, you can apply the principles of *Mian Xiang* on a larger scale, such as when dealing with personnel or strategic decision-making processes within private corporations and government bodies. When you have mastered the art of face reading, you will be in a much better position when negotiating deals, because you will know a lot about your opponent's character and potential beforehand, and this will enable you to tackle the people you are dealing with more effectively and to win their support.

1

The Shape of the Face

Yin and Yang, the Five Elements and the Ten Face Patterns

Yin and Yang

THE CHINESE TEND TO THINK of the whole universe in terms of the principles of yin and yang. To be strictly accurate, yin is thought of as the principle realized on earth, while yang is the principle realized in heaven. However, this pair of polarities can be applied to almost everything. Yin stands generally for the feminine principle: the ground, the female, the moon, the night, motherhood, softness, benevolence, water and so on. Yang, on the other hand, represents the heavens, the male, the sun, the day, fatherhood, strength, righteousness, fire and so on.

It is said in the ancient Chinese oracle, the *I Ching*, that yin standing alone will not yield, just as yang standing alone will not grow and prosper. From this saying evolves a Chinese divination rule known as 'left is for the man and right is for the woman'. Chinese fortune-tellers apply this rule in face reading and hand reading as well. Therefore, when reading a face, you should start from the left side for a man and the right for a woman.

The Five Elements

The concept of the five elements is an integral part of the Chinese philosophy of life. Whereas there are only four elements according to the traditional Western way of thinking, the ancient Chinese believed that everything in the universe was composed of the five elements of wood, fire, water, metal and earth. The principle of the five elements is fundamental to many aspects of traditional Chinese culture, including the fields of medicine, astrology, acupuncture, hand reading and *feng shui*, as well as the practice of face reading.

The relationships between these five elements can be either mutually productive or mutually destructive. In terms of being mutually productive, it is believed that water nourishes wood, wood feeds fire, fire produces earth, earth supplies metal and metal yields water. In this way the five elements complete a cycle of mutual production. In terms of being destructive, water quenches fire, fire melts metal, metal cuts wood,

wood dredges earth and earth blocks water, thus completing the cycle of mutual destruction.

Each of the five elements possesses certain characteristics and associations. Water is the most flexible, being able to permeate and sink to lower levels; fire is the most violent, because it burns and moves upward; wood is durable and resistant; metal is understood as being sharp and square in nature; and earth provides the working ground for all the other elements and is therefore thick and stable.

By using their strong insight and sharp observational skills, the Chinese established a list of correspondences between the elements, natural objects and social phenomena. These include, but are not limited to, tastes, smells, seasons of the year, colours, human organs and ethical values.

Element	Direction	Value	Feature	Organ	Colour	Season	Shape
Metal	West	Righteousness	Eye	Lung	White	Autumn	Square
Water	North	Intelligence	Mouth	Kidney	Black	Winter	Round
Wood	East	Kindness	Ears	Liver	Green	Spring	Oblong
Fire	South	Propriety	Forehead	Heart	Red	Summer	Pointed
Earth	Centre	Reliability	Nose	Spleen	Yellow	Mid-season	Thick

Table of the Five Elements and their Correspondences

A person's fate is dependent on the combination of these five elements in his or her face and body. The Chinese art of face reading distinguishes five main character groups. These five groups reflect the properties of the five elements.

METAL

'Metal' people have square faces (*see* fig. 1). They are usually very well built, with rounded bodies or curvaceous figures. They often appear elegant, and they achieve much in life. They enjoy success in mid-life, and will often have accumulated great wealth by their old age.

fig. 1

WATER

'Water' people often have rounded faces, with foreheads that are smaller than their chins (*see* fig. 2). Their fingers are tapered and small. Water people tend to be very careful and think long and hard before leaping. If they can try to be a little bit more aggressive and take the initiative more often, life will be much easier for them.

fig. 2

WOOD

'Wood' people generally have long faces (*see* fig. 3). Their bodies are slight yet tall, sometimes resembling a tree, and they tend to have dark skin-tones. They are usually philosophical and are deep thinkers. They may spend too much time thinking, although unfortunately not about money. Luckily, they usually manage to get by one way or another.

fig. 3

FIRE

'Fire' people usually have heads which are pointed at the top and thick at the base (*see* fig. 4). They tend to have small hands and big feet. They are effective achievers and can be very aggressive, but they are loyal and remain true to their goals. Life is full of excitement for these people.

fig. 4

EARTH

'Earth' people are strongly built with thick skin and broad faces (*see* fig. 5). They seem to have a lot of energy and are very productive, often having many children. They usually enjoy long and happy lives with their loved ones.

fig. 5

The Ten Face Patterns

In addition to the five element groups that characterize a person's physique, there are ten basic face patterns. These indicate personality as well as an individual's luck in life.

THE YAU PATTERN

– THE STRUGGLING CHAMPION

In the Yau pattern, the forehead is narrow and weak, but the chin is strong and well developed like the Chinese character 'Yau' (*see* fig. 6). This is actually not a bad pattern. Yau people may have to fight through life, but they will succeed in the end. This pattern is especially favourable for women.

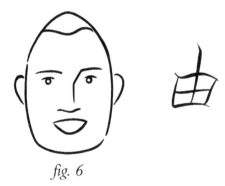

fig. 6

THE GAP PATTERN

– THE ACHIEVER

The Gap pattern (*see* fig. 7) is in some respects the reverse of Yau pattern. This pattern indicates someone pleasant and cultured, who gets through life smoothly until old age, when things may become difficult at times. This pattern can also indicate material or physical weakness, so it is very important that those with Gap-patterned faces pay particular attention to their health and finances when approaching their fifties. A woman with this face pattern is usually intelligent and may have lots of children.

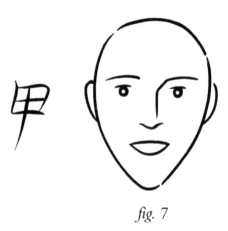

fig. 7

THE XUN PATTERN

– THE STRATEGIST

In this pattern, both the forehead and the chin are rather narrow and weak (*see* fig. 8), which indicates that the relationship between the person and his or her parents is rather poor. Many Xun people have to stand on their own two feet at an early age and have rather lonely childhoods. However, as they approach middle age, things will change in their favour. If these people work hard and keep their feet on the ground, their old age will be a good one.

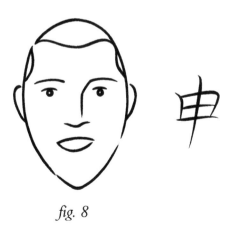

fig. 8

THE TIEN PATTERN

– THE EXECUTIVE

A person with the square Tien face pattern (*see* fig. 9) will lead a good life and will succeed in every aspect of life. Those Tien people who have dark complexions will enjoy good health, whereas those with pale skin will need to look after themselves carefully.

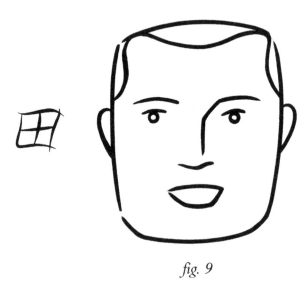

fig. 9

THE TUNG PATTERN

– THE SOCIAL SUCCESS

People with the rectangular Tung face pattern (*see* fig. 10) will lead good and prosperous lives. Women with this face pattern can expect to enjoy domestic bliss and to bear many children.

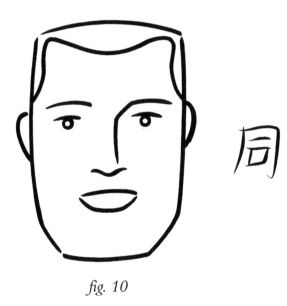

fig. 10

THE WANG PATTERN

– THE JOLLY GOOD FELLOW

In this face pattern, both the cheeks and the chin are very well developed (*see* fig. 11), indicating good health, but unfortunately not wealth. It is of vital importance for Wang people to realize that they must save some money to have security in their old age.

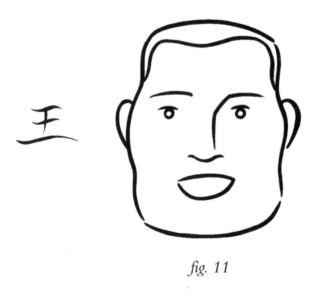

fig. 11

THE YUEN PATTERN

– THE OPTIMIST

Those with the round Yuen pattern (*see* fig. 12) may have had to leave home early in order to settle down far away from their parents. However, if Yuen people are willing to work hard, they will encounter no great problems in life. Also, if they have kind hearts and are willing to help others, good luck will come to them as a reward.

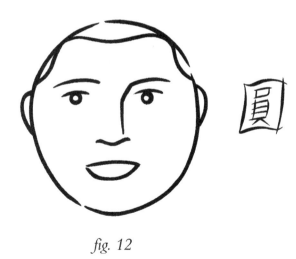

fig. 12

THE MU PATTERN

– THE STALWART

Like the Tung pattern, the Mu face pattern (*see* fig. 13) resembles a rectangle, but the chin is a little bit weaker than in a Tung person. The Mu pattern indicates long life, but good luck may disappear in old age. Therefore, it is very important for Mu people to try to help others and make friends when they themselves are prospering. Then, when they get old, they will get all the support they need.

fig. 13

THE YUNG PATTERN

– THE MISUNDERSTOOD

The Yung face pattern has a very strong and outstanding chin (*see* fig. 14). Those with this pattern can be rather rebellious, and they possess a strong sense of pride. As long as they are willing to show modesty, their luck will not vanish.

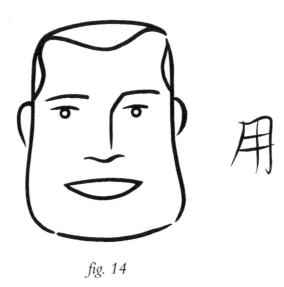

fig. 14

THE FENG PATTERN

– THE MID-LIFE CRISIS SUFFERER

The Feng face pattern has a well-developed forehead and a strong chin, but the middle part of the face is somewhat narrower (*see* fig. 15). Feng people can be moody and self-centred. Whatever their gender, those with the Feng pattern will be doomed to remain alone in life unless they are willing to improve their personal image.

fig. 15

2

The Regions of the Face

*The Four Regions, the Hundred Positions of the Floating Year,
the Five Mountains and the Planetary Points*

ACCORDING TO THE PRINCIPLES of *Mian Xiang*, the face can be mapped into various different areas. These separate regions relate to different ages as well as to different personality traits.

Regions Indicating Age

The Four Regions

The face can be divided into four basic regions, taking into account the principle of yin and yang: that is, 'left is for a man and right is for a woman'. These four regions divide the face into zones that correspond with particular ages (*see* fig. 16).

THE FIRST REGION

The first region relates to childhood issues, which are shown in the appearance of the ears. For men, the left ear corresponds with the childhood years between the ages of 1 and 7, and the right ear reveals the years between the ages of 8 and 14. The opposite is true for women. If the person being analysed is an adult, the ears reveal what has already happened to him or her; however, if you are reading the face of a child aged between 1 and 14, the ears will reveal what is happening at the present time.

THE SECOND REGION

The region of the forehead and the upper part of the face represents youth and early adulthood from the age of 15 until the age of 35. This region reveals whether a person will benefit from educational opportunities and parental support.

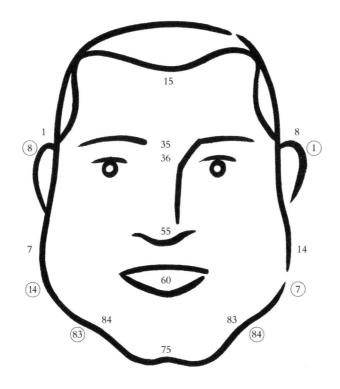

(The circled numbers show ages in relation to a man's face.)

fig. 16

THE THIRD REGION

The third, middle part of the face starts from the centre of the eyebrows and extends down to the tip of the nose. This region corresponds with the period of life between the ages of 35 and 55. Someone with well-structured eyebrows, intelligent eyes, strong and prominent cheeks and a strong, fleshy nose will be sure to enjoy a good and prosperous time during these years. In any event, a large nose indicates good fortune and the ability to make lots of money, although it has to be suited to the overall context of the face.

THE FOURTH REGION

The final, lower region of the face starts beneath the tip of nose and ends at the chin. This region relates to the period from the age of 56 until death. Someone with a pleasant, smiling mouth with pronounced laughter lines around it, good teeth and a strong chin will enjoy a pleasant and constructive old age.

The 100 Position Points of the Floating Year

The 100 Position Points of the Floating Year each represent a specific year between the ages of 1 and 100 (*see* fig. 17). By looking at a particular Position Point on the face, we can tell whether or not someone will be lucky at any given age.

Having read hundreds of thousands of faces and carried out extensive research, I have reached the conclusion that the standard Position Points on the Chinese Face Map used by many Chinese fortune-tellers need to be moved slightly to suit our modern times. My findings suggest that it would be wrong to follow blindly in the footsteps of earlier Chinese fortune-tellers.

LOCATING THE POSITION POINTS
OF THE FLOATING YEAR

The ancient Chinese masters believed that a person's lifespan should be measured from the moment of conception, but I think this has to be changed. According to my research, it is far more appropriate to measure lifespan from the time of birth. I have located the Position Point that corresponds with the age of 35 right between the eyes, and the Point indicating the age of 55 is on the very tip of the nose.

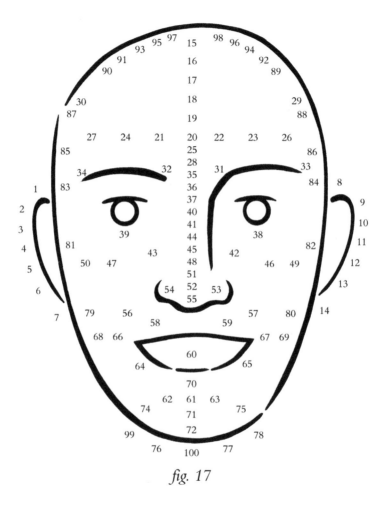

fig. 17

34

Regions Indicating Character

The Five Mountains

In addition to the Four Regions, the Chinese art of face reading divides the face into five different parts known as the Five Mountains (*see* fig. 18).

THE NORTH MOUNTAIN (Heng Shan)

– THE FOREHEAD

The North Mountain (Heng Shan) corresponds with the forehead, which indicates intelligence. If this area is well developed, it is a sure sign of someone who is very intelligent and full of ambition. He or she will have the chance to become well educated. However, if this area is injured or there are scars on it, the possessor will have to leave his or her own country at some point between the ages of 15 and 34 in order to make a living abroad.

THE SOUTH MOUNTAIN (Hang Shan)

– THE CHIN

The South Mountain (Hang Shan) is located at the chin, which indicates achievements and success. When this part is round and strong, the possessor will have achieved success by the end of his or her life, and will

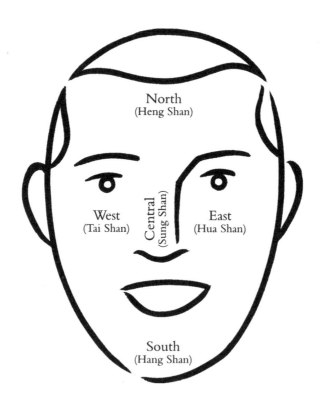

North
(Heng Shan)

West
(Tai Shan)

Central
(Sung Shan)

East
(Hua Shan)

South
(Hang Shan)

fig. 18

have obtained wealth and fame through his or her own efforts. But if this area is pointed and very weak, it suggests that the last part of life – usually from the ages of 70 to 100 years old – will be rather a poor period.

THE CENTRAL MOUNTAIN (Sung Shan)
– THE NOSE

The Central Mountain (Sung Shan) relates to the nose region, which indicates wealth and a person's ability to lead. A nose that is strong, straight and prominent suggests good health and good fortune. Just take a look at any person you meet: most people with a strong social standing have very strong, straight and prominent noses. The nose is very important for anyone who wants to succeed and become famous, and some people in the Far East and America will even have surgery in order to remedy any perceived flaws in this area.

THE EAST MOUNTAIN (Hua Shan) AND THE WEST
MOUNTAIN (Tai Shan) – THE TWO CHEEKS

The left cheek is the East Mountain (Hua Shan), and the right cheek is the West Mountain (Tai Shan); both mountains indicate power. When these parts are very well developed, they indicate someone with the will to strive for power. A person with well-formed East and West Mountains will relate easily to others and win the necessary support to succeed.

If all the mountains relate to each other in a harmonious way – that is, if they are well formed and are not too strong or too weak – it means that the person's life is in harmony, and a person whose life is in harmony will go far, according to principles of Mian Xiang.

The Planetary Points

There are five different planetary points on the face (*see* fig. 19). These relate to the heavenly bodies of Saturn, Jupiter, Venus, Mars and Mercury.

THE POINT OF SATURN

(THE EARTH STAR)

This point corresponds with the nose, and indicates a person's security and vitality. Ideally, the nose should be a little brownish in colour. If it is red, this means that the earth is burnt. When the earth is dried and burnt, there is no water, and water means money. Consequently, a person with a red nose might have some financial troubles, and this, of course, is not a favourable sign.

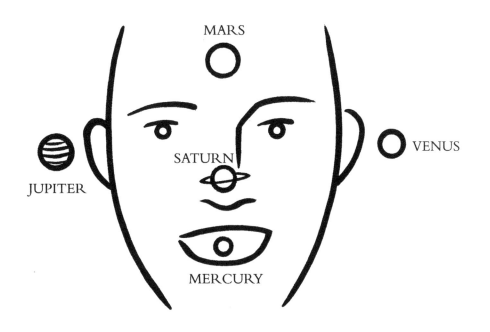

fig. 19

THE POINT OF JUPITER

(THE WOOD STAR)

The left ear represents this point. It indicates fortune and wisdom. The right colour for this point is pinkish-white; it should be lighter than the face. It is not a favourable sign for it to be too red or grey, as this can suggest health problems. If the left ear is turning either of those colours, the subject should visit the doctor.

THE POINT OF VENUS

(THE GOLD OR METAL STAR)

The right ear represents the Point of Venus. It indicates love and elegance, and the correct colour for it is a pinkish-white.

THE POINT OF MARS

(THE FIRE STAR)

The Point of Mars is represented by the forehead. When this part is wide and strong with a slightly reddish colour, it shows someone with intelligence who may hold an important position. Anyone who has a strong forehead possesses the potential to obtain high office in the public eye, perhaps in politics or military positions.

THE POINT OF MERCURY

(THE WATER STAR)

The mouth represents the Point of Mercury. It indicates wealth, vitality and flexibility, and the best colour for it is rosy red. Traditionally, a man should have a big mouth, as this denotes tolerance, bravery and ambition, and a woman should have a small mouth, as this indicates submissiveness. (However, as we will see in chapter 5, these traditional interpretations of mouth size are now being revised to reflect the new status of women in society.) Whatever the gender of the owner, the mouth should be tight-sitting when closed with the corners pointing upwards in a smile. The teeth should be clean and white, as this indicates a good diet and good health. With such a mouth, the money will just keep pouring in.

3

The Upper Part of the Face

The Ears, Forehead, Eyebrows and Eyes

The Ears

IN *MIAN XIANG*, WE ALWAYs start by reading the ears. This is because the ears are the first organs to develop in relation to a human face. As we saw in chapter 2, the ears account for the first fourteen years of life. For men, the left ear represents the period from 1 to 7 years of age, and the right ear represents the period from 8 to 14. For women, it is the opposite way round.

Chinese history contains many fascinating stories about heroes and what they looked like. Liu Bei (AD 160–223), the Emperor of the Shu kingdom, was believed to have ears that were so long that they touched his shoulders. According to the Chinese art of face reading, this signified that Liu Bei had the 'Mandate of Heaven': that is, the God-given authority to rule a nation. One of my own ancestors, General Chiang Kai-shek, also had long ears, which were flat and were positioned high on his head in relation to his extremely bushy eyebrows. He was the leader of the Chinese nationalists in China and later on in Taiwan until he passed away in his eighties.

Many have remarked on the appearance of Prince Charles's ears, both of which are quite fleshy and stick out. The first aspect – their fleshiness – indicates that the Prince comes from a very solid family background, but one which places a lot of demands on him that he is obliged to live up to. It also signals that he will inherit quite a lot of money from his family, something which would appear to be obviously true. The second aspect – the way in which they protrude – indicates that their owner is required to live according to a strict set of principles and standards. Every move he makes will be watched and his behaviour will be analysed. He will have had an especially sheltered childhood, and will have been taught to behave according to the exacting requirements of – in his case royal – etiquette.

The Position of the Ears

As a general rule, good ears are thick, long and flat with fleshy earlobes. Ideally, they should sit high on the head in relation to the eyebrows. High intelligence is indicated if they are situated higher than the eyebrows.

The Colour of the Ears

The colour of the ears also has a specific meaning. White and red are the best colours for the ears, as these two colours indicate intelligence and success. Black or dark shades are considered to have the opposite effect and are signs of bad health and an unhappy childhood. If the ears begin to turn dark, this warns of an approaching serious medical condition or even a legal problem.

The Shape of the Ears

Different shapes of ears reveal different qualities. They provide reliable clues about the personality and childhood years between the ages of 1 and 14.

METAL EARS

Metal Ears are strong, fleshy and white and sit tightly against the head (*see* fig. 20). They sit higher than the eyebrows, and the contours of the inner and outer ear ridges are very distinct from one another. This shape indicates high intelligence, possible national fame and a strong position in life. Metal Ears are also a sign of a happy childhood with a solid family background. Success can come very early, especially if the ears are set on the sides of either a Metal- or a Water-shaped face.

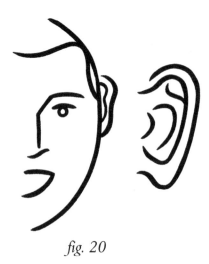

fig. 20

WATER EARS

Water Ears are fleshy, long and flat, with big fleshy earlobes that almost reach the shoulders (*see* fig. 21). Water ears indicate power, authority, wealth, honour and success. People with Water Ears have relatively good childhoods: they receive a lot of affection from their parents and are strongly protected by their families. If the face is of a Water or Metal shape, this is an especially good combination, indicating someone who may climb to the top in a political or military career. However, it will take time for the person to achieve this high status, and he or she may not do so until late in life.

fig. 21

WOOD EARS

Wood Ears are expansive and protruding (*see* fig. 22). They are wider at the top, with a more prominent outer ridge than inner ridge. Wood Ears are signs of wealth, intelligence and long life. Most people with Wood Ears are born into well-to-do families and possess artistic and aesthetic talents. These people do not need to worry about their lives, as they are born with silver spoons in their mouths. If they want to pursue a career in art or science, they have a very good chance of succeeding. Such ears are best set on a Wood- or Water-shaped face.

fig. 22

FIRE EARS

Fire Ears are the opposite of Water Ears: they are much wider at the bottom with more pointed tips (*see* fig. 23). Fire Ears denote intelligence, effectiveness, wealth and great success at a later stage in life. People with Fire Ears have very active childhoods, and their parents will generally let them do whatever they like; as a result, they tend to be quite independent at an early age. It is said that owners of Fire Ears will find themselves a devoted spouse, a harmonious family and a happy old age. However, they can also be bad-tempered, overcautious and very suspicious of others.

fig. 23

EARTH EARS

Earth Ears are long and fleshy with big earlobes that lean forward to the mouth as if protecting the face (*see* fig. 24). People with Earth Ears usually have very solid childhoods, in which they are given the time and support they need to make plans for their futures. Owners of Earth Ears can reach the top in government positions, as long as the other parts of the face are well proportioned. They are earthy types, and are great lovers of both food and the opposite sex. They are born lucky, as they will have plenty to eat and will find it easy to attract romantic attention.

fig. 24

In addition to these five traditional ear types, I would like to introduce some other types of ear that I have identified.

MOUSE EARS

Mouse Ears are small in size, somewhat protruding and pointed at the top (*see* fig. 25). They reveal that the owner had a difficult childhood because of either family troubles or health problems. Those with Mouse Ears can be bad-tempered, sometimes even to the point of bitterness; they can also be calculating and opportunistic. Happily, as I have said before, our faces have the tendency to keep on changing, and our ears and noses never stop growing. This means that we have the chance of making a better life for ourselves by special efforts and hard work, whatever the shape of our ears.

fig. 25

PIG EARS

Pig Ears are large in size but thin and soft, with the whole ear protruding forward and lacking distinctive inner ear ridges (*see* fig. 26). Those with Pig Ears will have to work hard to make ends meet. They will have to reckon with many ups and downs in life, and one thing is for sure: nothing will come free of charge for people with this kind of ear.

fig. 26

EARS WITH WIDE DOORS

If the ear entrance is wider than the width of one finger, it is considered to be a Wide Door (*see* fig. 27). People with such ears are often intelligent, generous and open-minded. In other words, they are very receptive to external influences and new ideas. Because of their positive attitude, they tend to be long-lived and lead very enjoyable lives.

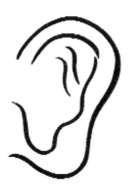

fig. 27

53

EARS WITH NARROW DOORS

If the ear entrance is narrower than the width of a finger, it is considered to be a Narrow Door (*see* fig. 28). This indicates that the owner is conservative, stingy and narrow-minded. People with this shape of ear tend to be very negative and worry so much that their lives may be shortened by anxiety.

fig. 28

EARS WITH BIG EARLOBES

These ears are fleshy with long earlobes that almost reach the shoulders (*see* fig. 29). They denote good luck, a happy destiny and a fulfilling sex life. People with big earlobes are very lucky in family life with satisfactory spouses. They may have many sexual partners in the course of their lives: they are bound to marry more than once, and they may even have extramarital affairs.

fig. 29

EARS WITH SMALL EARLOBES

The opposite of big earlobes is, of course, small earlobes (*see* fig. 30). If the earlobes are thin and short, they are considered to be small. This kind of shape can denote misfortune in relationships and an unfulfilling sex life. Owners of such ears often have a distant and difficult relationship with their parents, and they may lead a very lonely life, even at an early age. They will have to work hard later in life in order to get by.

fig. 30

RECTANGULAR EARS

Ears that are more or less rectangular in shape indicate intelligence, wealth, high social status and a big family (*see* fig. 31). This is a good shape.

fig. 31

EARS WITH PROMINENT RIDGES

There are usually two ridges in an ear: the inner ridge and the outer ridge. In *Mian Xiang*, we say that the inner ridge stands for vitality and ambition, while the outer one stands for wisdom and good health. It is therefore quite obvious that a good ear should have prominent inner and outer ridges. People with such ears will be wise, highly ambitious and full of vitality and self-confidence (*see* fig. 32).

fig. 32

The Forehead

Now that we have considered the ears, we can turn to the forehead. The forehead occupies the space between the hairline at the top of the face and the middle of the eyebrows.

The forehead represents character, which is the yang (masculine) aspect of the face. As we saw in chapter 2, the forehead indicates the owner's intelligence and educational possibilities. It is especially relevant as an indication of the relationship between the person and his or her parents.

In chapter 2, we saw that the forehead can be referred to as a Mountain, and that it should therefore be strong and prominent. Furthermore, the forehead represents the planet Mars, so the best colour for it is pinkish. Ideally, it ought to glow and shine. Wrinkles or lines on the forehead indicate experiences. Positive and good experiences are shown by straight, unbroken lines or wrinkles. Negative and bad experiences are shown by lines or wrinkles that are crooked and broken.

The Shape of the Forehead

There are three basic shapes of forehead: the square, the rounded and the tapered.

SQUARE FOREHEAD

A square and high forehead (*see* fig. 33) indicates good intellectual ability and excellent values, accompanied by a fine family background and good mental power.

A forehead that is square and fairly high indicates a person with a strong intellect, sound practical instincts and the necessary background and education to be successful in middle-management positions.

If the forehead is square and short, the owner will have a bad start in life, but a good measure of common sense and good character will ensure that he or she finds the abilities to get by.

fig. 33

ROUNDED FOREHEAD

A high and rounded forehead with no scars (*see* fig. 34) indicates a peaceful and friendly nature. This belongs to those who come from good backgrounds and have pleasant childhoods. These people are not usually very interested in achieving prominence: they are satisfied with what they already have.

A forehead that is rounded and fairly high suggests a very timid person who is content with an average life and who will not make much effort to alter the situation into which he or she was born.

A forehead that is rounded but somewhat low often indicates

fig. 34

someone who has got off to a poor start in life; however, if the other parts of the face are well developed, he or she will be able to attain a position of security in later years.

TAPERED FOREHEAD

A narrow, tapered forehead (*see* fig. 35) is commonly seen on a Fire-type person. If the forehead is high, this signals a very adventurous person. If it is low, this indicates a person who is very impulsive but lacking in intellectual power.

fig. 35

The Contour of the Forehead

There are four basic types of contour to the forehead.

STRAIGHT

A forehead that appears high, straight and flat when observed from the side, and which extends straight down from the hairline to the browbone (*see* fig. 36), indicates a person with a strong character and intellectual power. However, this person may become very fixed in his or her views at an early age, disliking change and wanting stability.

fig. 36

When the forehead is straight and flat but rather low, the owner will have to work hard to get by in his or her younger years. For such a person, nothing will come free of charge.

DOMED

If the forehead is domed, rounded and full from the side view (*see* fig. 37), the owner is a strong person who has the ability to make adjustments to meet life's challenges.

fig. 37

SLOPING

A sloping forehead (*see* fig. 38) indicates a person who is somewhat restless, and who may be adventurous in a reckless manner.

fig. 38

BULGING

If the forehead bulges from the hairline (*see* fig. 39), the owner possesses excessive drive and a strong intellect which may seem slightly out of kilter with reality, but which may lead to success and great achievements after certain efforts.

fig. 39

The Eyebrows

Human beings are the only creatures on earth who are equipped with such informative tools as the eyebrows. Through these, we can signal our emotions to those around us. They reveal whether we are happy, surprised or sad; if we are happy, the eyebrows will rise, and if we are discontented, they will sit low and may even wrap together in the middle.

In *Mian Xiang*, the eyebrows are believed to indicate general character and the way in which we relate to our surroundings. They reveal much about our relationships with our parents and siblings, and also about our aspirations. For men, the left brow is called the Baron and the right one is the Counsellor. It is vice versa for women. Ideally, the brows should be the same size and shape, as this indicates balance within the person's character: authority (the Baron) is balanced by wisdom (the Counsellor), and this means that the person's authority is applied wisely. In some faces, the eyebrows may not be identical, which indicates that the individual will either be rash in his or her application of authority or too cautious to apply authority boldly.

Personal reputation and good name are important to us all, and the eyebrows reveal the extent to which we are esteemed by those around us. Anyone dealing with the arts, showmanship, politics or anything that brings them before the public eye will need to have distinctive eyebrows. It is no wonder that the famous opera-singer Pavarotti insists that extra colour is applied to his already very distinctive eyebrows before a performance, just so that he can get an even better effect from them. The statesmen Joseph Stalin and Leonid Brezhnev both had very distinctive eyebrows that more or less joined up in the middle. This sign of bravery and ruthlessness often appears on the faces of dictators and those with military connections. Zhou En Lai had similarly prominent eyebrows, but luckily they did not join up in the middle: he was loved by the Chinese people and was a good administrator in the new China. On the other hand, Lin Biu, who was one of the most famous generals in Mao's army, also had very prominent eyebrows; however, when he tried to stage a coup d'état against Mao Tse Tung, he failed, and his plane was shot down over Mongolia under the orders of Zhou En Lai.

General Indications

Here are some more general guidelines about the ways in which eyebrows can reveal personality traits:

- Dark and heavy brows indicate one who is demanding but effective.

- If the eyebrow is thick and dark and the hairs point in lots of different directions (*see* fig. 40), the owner will have to deal with unexpected setbacks from time to time.

fig. 40

- Smooth, well-shaped brows indicate controlled emotions, sexual fidelity and pleasant relationships.

- Thin and well-defined eyebrows that are light in colour (*see* fig. 41) indicate a person who is calm and peace-loving. This person likes to avoid hard work: when confronted by a problem, he or she will try to get through it in a smooth and quiet way.

fig. 41

- Thin, light brows reveal someone who is flexible and very amenable, particularly in affairs of the heart.

- Light, shaggy brows with unruly hairs are indicators of sexual promiscuity.

- Long hairs appearing within the brow after the age of 40 are signs of a long life.

- Eyebrow hairs that point upwards within the eyebrow (*see* fig. 42) reveal that the owner is brave and opinionated. They can also indicate a hot temper and someone who tends to speak before thinking.

fig. 42

- Hairs in the outer tip of the brow pointing upwards indicate help from family and circumstances.

- Eyebrow hairs that point downwards (*see* fig. 43) belong to people who are slightly nervous and lacking in confidence: they are always willing to seek compromises and to avoid confrontation.

fig. 43

- If the hair at the top of the eyebrow points downwards and those on the bottom point upwards so that they meet in the middle (*see* fig. 44), it is an indication that this person worries too much, often unnecessarily.

- A strong and well-developed eyebrow bone is a sign of courage and individuality. If the bones are extremely pronounced, the owner may also be rather aggressive.

- A prominent bone situated just beneath the eyebrows indicates fame of a noble nature.

fig. 44

The Shape of the Eyebrows

In this section, I hope to teach you how to analyse the various different types of eyebrow shapes. However, you may have to mix and match these guidelines in order to interpret the eyebrow shapes that you encounter.

LONG EYEBROWS

If the eyebrows are longer than the eye itself, the hairs lie in the same direction, and the eyebrow has a nice, glossy appearance (*see* fig. 45), a good thinker is indicated. This type of eyebrow normally belongs to someone very intellectual who is a talented speaker. This person is usually on friendly terms with family, friends and colleagues. He or she will make many friends and get lots of support.

fig. 45

SHORT EYEBROWS

In Short Eyebrows, the hairs of the eyebrows appear rough and uneven, and the eyebrows look shorter than the eye (*see* fig. 46), indicating someone who is likely to come from a small family. This person may have problems sustaining a good relationship with loved ones. He or she may have a bad temper and get into arguments.

fig. 46

BIG EYEBROWS

These eyebrows are wide, long and well formed (*see* fig. 47). They indicate those who are not afraid of dealing with difficulties. These people are brave and will speak out in support of others. They may be very dominant and always have the final word in relationship matters.

fig. 47

EYEBROWS RESEMBLING THE
CHINESE CHARACTER 'ONE'

This shape is straightforward to identify: it looks like the Chinese character for 'One' (*see* fig. 48). The hairs are thick, and the roots are strong. This type of eyebrow usually belongs to people who come from large families in which the members maintain close relationships with one another. They will do good business at an early age and will enjoy a good reputation at work. This shape also denotes a strong and lasting marriage.

fig. 48

GHOST EYEBROWS

The Ghost Eyebrow is situated on the lower part of the eyebrow bone. It is curved in shape and rather short in length (*see* fig. 49). The hairs do not follow the flow of the curve but point upwards and lie straight. This type of eyebrow denotes those who find it hard to trust other people and who are suspicious of others' motives. People with Ghost Eyebrows may also be introverts who prefer to keep their thoughts private. They will have problems finding a suitable career or a romantic partner with whom they feel comfortable and who takes them seriously.

fig. 49

SHARP KNIFE EYEBROWS

The shape of this eyebrow resembles a dagger (*see* fig. 50). It has a sharp head and broadens at the end. The hairs are strong and thick. It belongs to natural-born businessmen and women, who rarely miss the opportunity to make a profit or gain an advantage. When faced with a problem, these people are good at finding the easiest way out. They are always confident and happy to tell others about their successes and conquests.

fig. 50

CIRCULAR, ROLLING EYEBROWS

In this shape, the hairs are thick and all curl in the same direction (see fig. 51). This is a very special eyebrow and is frequently seen on the faces of powerful leaders, such as generals.

fig. 51

BROOM EYEBROWS

A broom eyebrow is one in which the hairs are thick at the beginning of the eyebrow but widen out to become scattered and scarce at the end, like a broom (*see* fig. 52). This kind of eyebrow usually belongs to those who come from large families in which the contact between family members is very poor. Distance and financial problems prevent them from helping each other. Although those with broom eyebrows do manage on their own, they are never likely to be wealthy.

fig. 52

SWORD EYEBROWS

In this shape, the eyebrow grows on the upper part of the eyebrow bone and is straight, long, wide and almost flat (*see* fig. 53). The hairs all point in the same direction, and the eyebrow is thicker at the end. This shape denotes those possessed of very good judgement.

fig. 53

FINE AND DELICATE EYEBROWS

This type of eyebrow is long and slightly curved, almost like a bridge (*see* fig. 54). The hairs all point in the same direction, and the roots cannot be seen clearly. This indicates trustworthy people who can be relied upon. When confronted with a problem, this kind of person will always be willing to find a peaceful compromise. He or she will treat family and friends fairly, which brings them good fortune in both career and family life.

fig. 54

The Eyes

The eyes have been called 'the windows of the soul'. They are therefore very important features that have to be taken into account by a master of *Mian Xiang*. In many respects, no other part of the face reveals more about a person's personality and destiny than the eyes. Happily, if the eyes are of a fortunate shape, the person will have a chance to make a success of life even if the other parts of the face are less fortunate.

Even the direction of the gaze is significant. Those whose gaze is always directed above the head of the person they are talking to are proud and arrogant individuals. People who look downwards are timid and cautious. If a person tries to avoid looking at you, casting his or her gaze here and there instead, this speaks of someone who is bound to have some ulterior motive: he or she could be either trying to steal something or intending to harm someone sexually. In other circumstances, a person who dares not look straight into your eyes while facing you is someone with a guilty conscience. Straightforward eye contact reveals a person who is intelligent and brave. However, such individuals may have very high opinions of themselves and be rather proud people who do not think much of others.

Those with big eyes are emotional and artistic types, whereas those with small eyes tend to be more fastidious and cautious. The latter like to do some research and have time to reflect before making decisions. Eyes that sit deeply in the face denote a person who has deep thoughts. Eyes that bulge out indicate a person who has lots of energy and who tends to be impulsive and restless. Irrespective of the colour of the iris, the different shapes of the eye reveal a great deal about the personality of their owner.

The Shape of the Eyes

DRAGON EYES

In Dragon Eyes, the irises are large, and both the irises and the whites of the eyes are very vivid and marked (*see* fig. 55). People with Dragon Eyes are very strong and self-assured, and they have a lot of energy. These people are popular among their friends and colleagues, particularly because of their sympathetic natures. Those with this shape of eye are always ready to come to the aid of those who need help. They are very artistic and creative, and they approach their work with great enthusiasm.

fig. 55

LION EYES

Lion Eyes are very large, and the irises and whites are sharply distinct from one another (*see* fig. 56). The iris is always positioned towards the top, and the lid is folded with several lines. This eye type indicates someone who is very serious and capable of reaching a high position in life. People with Lion Eyes take full responsibility for whatever they choose to do. Their judgement is respected by people around them.

fig. 56

OXEN EYES

In Oxen Eyes, the colours of the iris and the white are very bright and vivid (*see* fig. 57). The eyes are huge but do not protrude. Those with Oxen Eyes enjoy a relaxed and gentle attitude to life. It is very unusual for them to be bothered by emotional outbursts. The wrinkles found above and beneath such eyes indicate a very trustworthy character who fulfils his or her promises.

fig. 57

HORSE EYES

The lower lid is folded, and the upper lid is soft. The wrinkles at the outer corner of the eye point downwards. The eye itself is slightly bulging and a little bit wet (*see* fig. 58). Horse Eyes belong to those who are energetic and active, although their efforts will not always be rewarded as they might like. In order to achieve what they want, those with Horse Eyes will have to persevere, whatever professional or personal setbacks they may encounter.

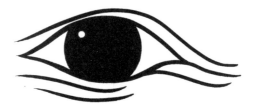

fig. 58

Eyelashes

- Long eyelashes reveal their owner to be soft-hearted, sensitive and spiritual in nature.

- Short eyelashes indicate a strong and rather bad-tempered person.

- Thin and loose or sparse lashes indicate a person who is inactive and sluggish or who has poor energy circulation.

4

The Middle Part of the Face

The Nose, Philtrum and Cheeks

The Nose

ACCORDING TO *MIAN XIANG*, the nose represents the region of humanity, as it is positioned in the middle part of the face between the forehead, which represents heaven, and the chin, which represents earth. The nose is therefore a very important part of the face. As we saw in chapter 2, the nose also represents middle age, from the age of 35 at the top of the nose down to the age of 55 at the tip of the nose. The nose is associated with health and wealth, so those people who are fortunate enough to have nice, well-proportioned noses will be prosperous and lucky during this particular period of life.

The Bridge of the Nose

Many Chinese people believe that people with a high and straight nose bridge will automatically enjoy high social standing. The truth of this belief can easily be verified by observing the noses of celebrities worldwide. Just take a look at Bill Gates, Bill Clinton, John F. Kennedy, Margaret Thatcher, Tony Blair, Richard Branson, Zhu Rong Zhi and Albert Einstein. All these people have shaped our world and will continue to influence our lives for many years to come.

If a man has a high and straight nose bridge, it is said that his wife will be very pretty and helpful. Similarly, if a woman has a very pleasing and proportionate nose bridge, she is sure to be blessed with a handsome husband who holds a high position in life.

The Nose Tip and Outer Nostrils

While the height of the nose bridge reveals its owner's social standing, the size of the nose tip and its two outer nostrils (the wing-like bumps covering the nostrils) provide information about the person's financial fortunes (*see* fig. 59). The nose tip is an indication of how easily a person can make money, and the outer nostrils are metaphorical banks in which to stash the hard-earned cash. Just look at the nose of the chief of the central American Bank, Mr Greenspan, who has a high nose bridge, a fleshy nose tip and strong outer nostrils. With this man and his nose at the top, it is no wonder that the USA has enjoyed economic prosperity recently, with a minimum of unemployment.

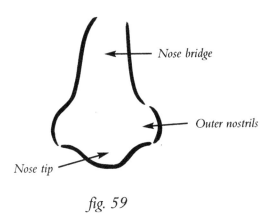

fig. 59

The Shape of the Nose

DRAGON NOSE

The Dragon Nose has a long, high and straight bridge, with a strong fleshy tip and large outer nostrils, although the nostrils themselves are relatively small (see fig. 60). This kind of shape indicates that the owner has great power, wealth and an attractive spouse.

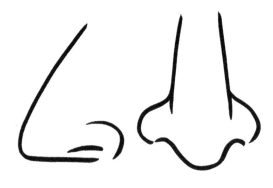

fig. 60

RHINOCEROS NOSE

The shape of the Rhinoceros Nose seems to extend straight into the forehead without a break (*see* fig. 61). The nose bridge is very high and straight, and the nose has a fleshy, round tip. The Chinese think this is a very fortunate nose shape. The owner is bound to be a leader, probably in politics or the military. Throughout the ages, many famous heads of state and great soldiers have possessed such an auspicious nose.

fig. 61

LION NOSE

The Lion Nose has a relatively low bridge coupled with a strong, fleshy nose tip and outer nostrils (*see* fig. 62). This kind of nose indicates extraordinary power, wealth and success. However, that success will not come easily, as those possessing a Lion Nose will have to fight for their achievements much more than those with Dragon Noses or Rhinoceros Noses.

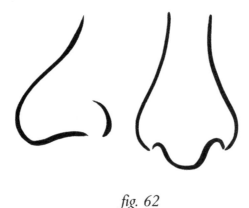

fig. 62

TIGER NOSE

The shape of the Tiger Nose is very similar to that of the Rhinoceros Nose, as both of them have a very high bridge going straight into the forehead (*see* fig. 63). The only difference is that a Tiger Nose has a wider bridge and smaller outer nostrils. The owner of a Tiger Nose will possess very strong intuitive skills, courage and a desire to get to the top. People born with such a nose will never stop fighting, and they are capable of great deeds in times of both war and peace.

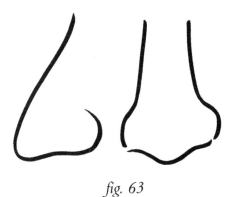

fig. 63

GARLIC NOSE

The Garlic Nose has a very full and meaty tip at the end of a small, short nose bridge; it resembles a bulb of garlic in shape (*see* fig. 64). This nose is very similar to the Lion Nose, although the Garlic Nose has much wider outer nostrils. This nose denotes great material wealth, which will be gained through hard work after middle age. Those with such a nose are usually very good at making money and possess a strong business sense. However, in *Mian Xiang*, a Lion Nose is actually much preferable to a Garlic Nose.

fig. 64

COW NOSE

The Cow Nose has a short bridge and a round tip with meaty outer nostrils and hidden inner nostrils (*see* fig. 65). Such a nose signifies wealth and artistic taste as well as diligence and a sense of logic. Most people with this kind of nose are self-made. Wealth and success will come slowly but surely to them, as will domestic bliss.

fig. 65

EAGLE NOSE

The Eagle Nose has the same shape as the beak of an eagle. It is high and arched, and the nose tip is sharply hooked and pointed, falling almost beneath the level of the nostrils (*see* fig. 66). People with such a nose are very cunning, shrewd and determined. They can reach high social positions, especially in politics and business. They will not hesitate to step on others in order to get what they want. They are never especially loyal towards their spouse or their friends.

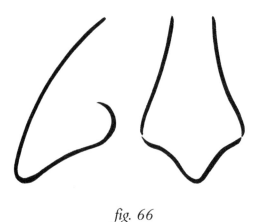

fig. 66

MONKEY NOSE

The Monkey Nose has one or several bumps along its bridge (*see* fig. 67). Such a nose indicates financial and relationship troubles, especially during the period from 36 years old to 55 years old. It also signifies health problems and a lonely character. People with such a nose risk getting divorced, going bankrupt or suffering from illness during middle age if they are not careful.

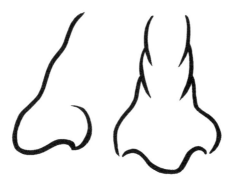

fig. 67

TWISTED NOSE

A Twisted Nose has one or several twists in the bridge, making the bones prominent (*see* fig. 68). Such a nose denotes dishonesty in intention, thinking and motivation. It also indicates frustration in money, relationships and career. If the nose tip is meaty, the owner cares about nothing but money. A pointed nose tip indicates a very opportunistic person who would not hesitate to step on others in order to achieve his or her goals.

fig. 68

GOAT NOSE

The Goat Nose has a superfluous fleshy bit with a split in it, which hangs down from the nose tip beneath the nostrils (*see* fig. 69). It denotes a lewd person who is sexually greedy and has a selfish nature. People with such a nose are usually very lucky with the opposite sex, but this nose does not bode well for their family lives. In other words, people with this shape of nose have too much sexual drive, and this makes them behave irrationally. They are often caught in love-triangle situations and may risk their own skin. (If you are thinking along the same lines as me, Bill Clinton will have sprung to your mind!)

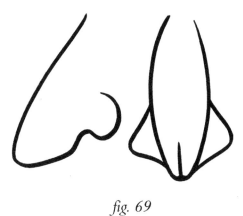

fig. 69

The Nostrils

It is the Chinese understanding that nostril openings are better hidden than exposed when the face is looked at levelly from the front. Exposed nostrils suggest that the owner has a poor understanding of modesty and tact. According to my own research, this is quite correct; also, a lot of people with exposed nostrils spend more money unnecessarily than those with hidden nostrils.

The shape of the nostril openings also has significance: here are the meanings of some of the basic shapes of nostril opening. (By the way, the best way to observe the shape of your own nostril openings is to look down into a mirror.)

- Round openings indicate originality and the ability to solve problems, but usually the owner will prefer to take shortcuts than to make long-term plans (*see* fig. 70).

fig. 70

- Oval openings indicate a daring, adventurous and innovative person (*see* fig. 71).

fig. 71

- Square nostril openings tell of a person who is stable and secure, and who sees projects through to their conclusions (*see* fig. 72).

fig. 72

- Triangular nostril openings show that the owner is careful or even stingy with money and is not too considerate in relationships (*see* fig. 73).

fig. 73

The Philtrum

The part that is located vertically between the nose and the upper lip is called the philtrum (*see* fig. 74). It is referred to as 'the Centre of Man' (*Renzhong*) in both Chinese acupuncture and *Mian Xiang*. The philtrum reveals vital information about the owner's health, social position, longevity and family.

Criteria for analysing the philtrum are based on the length, depth, coverage and symmetry of this interesting part of the face. In men, the philtrum should ideally be covered by the beard, as this is a sign of masculinity and authority. Men with uncovered philtrums tend to lack authority and have difficulty in gaining the support of those around them.

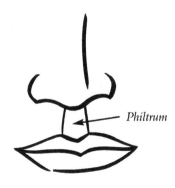

Philtrum

fig. 74

LONG, DEEP PHILTRUM

A good philtrum should be long and deep: in men, it should be covered with a beard as shown (*see* fig. 75). This means that the owner will be blessed with profound knowledge, a high social position, power, good health, a long life and a large family.

fig. 75

SHORT, FLAT PHILTRUM

This formation (*see* fig. 76) reveals someone who may come from a low social position and who experiences frustration in his or her career. People with such philtrums have relatively short lifespans and families with few children. It is a particularly bad sign if the philtrum is not only flat, but also dark and dim. If this is the case, the owner could be exposed to an accident unless he or she is careful; alternatively, he or she could be attacked by illness that is caused by leading a reckless life.

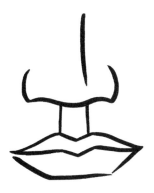

fig. 76

PARALLEL PHILTRUM

A parallel philtrum has the same width from top to bottom (*see* fig. 77). Such a philtrum indicates administrative talent and diplomatic skills.

fig. 77

WIDE-TOPPED PHILTRUM

Another interesting type of philtrum is one that is wide in the upper portion but narrows towards the bottom (*see* fig. 78). Such a philtrum is spoken of as having 'a Head like a Tiger but a Tail like a Snake'. This kind of philtrum indicates a fine start for the owner but a poor finish in later life. In other words, the owner of such a philtrum will have a happy youth, but things might go wrong in later years unless sufficient care is taken.

fig. 78

WIDE-BOTTOMED PHILTRUM

The most common type of philtrum is wider at the bottom than at the top (*see* fig. 79). This kind of philtrum denotes maturity and presence of mind: the owner will grow in knowledge as he or she advances in age. Wealth, knowledge and experience will come slowly but at a steady pace. The owner will also marry at a relatively late stage of life.

Whatever the shape of the philtrum, the appearance of a mole on it is

fig. 79

always significant. For example, a mole situated in the middle of the philtrum indicates a person who may experience reproductive problems, especially if this person is female. (For more information about interpreting moles, see chapter 6.)

The Cheekbones

In *Mian Xiang*, the cheekbones are thought of as the base of power. Prominent cheekbones are a sign of obtaining power: people with such cheekbones will find themselves in a powerful position accidentally at some point in life. However, in order to maintain that position, tact and diplomacy are called for. Cheekbones that are covered in flesh and look very rounded indicate that the owner will be able to maintin his or her power.

Measuring the scope and level of the cheekbones will reveal whether a person has power at home or in society. Cheekbones also denote personal authority and physical courage. Their appearance can be related to the types of physique associated with the five elements.

METAL

A Metal person tends to have a well-structured base to his or her cheekbones, showing power exerted through authority (*see* fig. 80).

fig. 80

WATER

A Water person may not appear to have cheekbones at all, because they will be covered up by lots of flesh (*see* fig. 81). However, the cheekbones will still be there, although hard to detect. This suggests a very diplomatic person who often exerts power behind the scenes so that the effect is felt but not seen.

fig. 81

WOOD

In a Wood person, the cheekbones are not very prominent: the lower part of the cheekbone tends to be rather flat, although the upper part of the cheekbone will be slightly higher (*see* fig. 82). Wood people often achieve great authority, but they have a tendency to exert less power than is required of them: they prefer to let others take the decisions.

fig. 82

FIRE

A Fire person has very strong, pointed cheekbones that are well covered with flesh (*see* fig. 83). Fire people are ambitious and aggressive, and are willing to use force if necessary in order to get things done. They make good leaders and pioneers, because they excel at tasks which require a lot of courage and energy.

fig. 83

EARTH

An Earth person would have a flatter base to the cheekbones, though the structure itself may be very visible (*see* fig. 84). This indicates a person who has power under control.

fig. 84

The Three Types of Cheekbone

There are many kinds of cheekbones to look out for, but broadly speaking there are three main types. These are high cheekbones, cheekbones connected to the ears, and low, receding cheekbones.

HIGH CHEEKBONES

High cheekbones are situated prominently on the face. They may be fleshy and round, like two guards protecting the face, or they may stand high to protect the nose (*see* fig. 85). Such cheekbones denote extraordinary courage, perseverance, strong willpower and political authority.

People with high cheekbones are often noted for their strong fighting spirit, aggression and adventurousness. It is therefore little wonder that many people holding high political or military office have very high cheekbones. Many great soldiers throughout history have been born with high and strong cheekbones. Consider Julius Caesar, Emperor Tai Zhong, Genghis Khan, Kublai Khan, Emperor Kangxi, Napoleon Bonaparte, Sir Winston Churchill, and Deng Xiaoping: all of them had very prominent cheekbones.

The famous Chinese general Li Guan, who served during the rule of the Emperor Wu Di in the Han dynasty, was an upstanding man of extraordinary bravery and military talent. He was given the name of the 'Flying General' and was credited with driving out the Huns.

fig. 85

However, for all his bravery and great deeds, he hardly received any reward or promotion from Emperor Wu Di, and he died a disillusioned and disappointed man. It is said that Li Guan was born with a pair of very prominent cheekbones, but he is also said to have had small eyes and a little nose, and these may have been the cause of his downfall.

Clearly, then, it is not enough just to have high and strong cheekbones to be successful in politics or in the military. They must be accompanied by a high nose and auspicious eyes. If the cheekbones are prominent but the nose is small and the eyes withdrawn, the owner cannot hope to get very far in these fields, and he or she is likely to experience many ups and downs.

Although possessing high cheekbones may mean having courage and power in the right circumstances, they are nevertheless not without their own drawbacks. Owners of high cheekbones are sometimes too power-orientated, aggressive and bad-tempered. This may damage their image and popularity, although they do not seem to worry about that much, for many of these people prefer to be feared rather than loved.

It is usually difficult to deal with people with high, strong cheekbones. Consequently, most Chinese men prefer to marry women with low cheekbones, in order not to be bossed around. A woman with strong, high cheekbones is said to be bossy, controlling and bad-tempered. When seen from the traditional Chinese perspective, such a personality certainly signals nothing but problems for the family. A woman with high cheekbones is said to be unlikely to have a happy marriage. She is thought to be likely to marry more than once, either because of divorce

fig. 86

or because her husband dies early. However, many successful women in modern times possess exactly this kind of cheekbone: just look at Margaret Thatcher. In fact, these days, high cheekbones in the female face can be considered an auspicious sign. They indicate that the woman may be very successful in her career and can lead a very happy family life, as long as her partner does not possess the same strength of character. If he does, the match will be rather strenuous.

CHEEKBONES CONNECTED TO THE EARS

Cheekbones that extend all the way to the ears (*see* fig. 86) are a sure sign of a reckless and fearless leader, a person who is willing to kill and take revenge. Such people lust for power, and in many cases they would rather physically destroy challengers to their power than win the battle and spare them. As we saw with the high cheekbones, however, these cheekbones will have to be accompanied by a high nose and good eyes if the owner is to obtain lasting high status.

LOW, RECEDING CHEEKBONES

Low, receding cheekbones (*see* fig. 87) denote exactly the opposite qualities to those shown by high cheekbones. Those with low, receding cheekbones prefer not to compete: they are more easily satisfied with the status quo and

fig. 87

will try to sort things out in a peaceful way. Their philosophy is to go with the flow, and sometimes they can even wear down a strong enemy with their mild but consistent tactics. It would be a big mistake to undervalue the capacity of these people for endurance and passive resistance.

5

The Lower Part of the Face

The Mouth, the Teeth, Laughter Lines and the Chin

The Mouth

THE MOUTH IS VERY IMPORTANT in the Chinese art of face reading, as it performs two vital functions – eating and communicating. To a large extent, it also determines our health, our success and our relationships with the people around us. As the commander of communication, the mouth can promote or destroy a relationship in a moment.

The Lips

THE COLOUR OF THE LIPS

Colour is a very important consideration when analysing the mouth: it reflects the owner's health and relationships with those around him or her. Criteria regarding the colour of the lips are more or less universal: they are applicable to virtually all ethnic groups except certain peoples from Africa and Australia.

Rosy lips denote good health, an optimistic attitude towards life and good relationships with others. White or dark lips are signs of ill health, pessimism and strained relationships with others. In other words, people with rosy lips often have more friends than those with dark-coloured or white lips. This is partly because those with rosy lips tend to be outgoing people who make friends easily.

THE SYMMETRY OF THE LIPS

It is said that if the upper lip is longer than the lower one, the owner's father will die before his or her mother. The opposite is thought to be true if the upper lip is shorter than the lower lip. Of course, if both lips are of the same length, both parents should have the same span of life.

THE THICKNESS OF THE LIPS

Generally speaking, thin lips indicate conservatism and determination. Those with thin lips are often not very good at expressing their feelings, although they are otherwise very articulate. They can be overly decisive and can often be considered cold-blooded by others. Reason and logic are their governing characteristics, and their chief goal is to obtain profit.

If the upper lip is thin and the lower is of normal thickness, the owner has a good head for business. If the upper lip is of a normal thickness, but the lower lip is thin, a tricky and unreliable person is indicated.

If both lips are thick, the person is honest, straightforward, loyal and hot-blooded. Such a person may be rather awkward in speech but will be rich in feelings and affection. The only drawback experienced by those with thick lips is that they have a tendency to hand themselves over to emotion and excessive sexual indulgence. Thick lips can signal great sexual appetite.

The Shape of the Mouth

When analysing the shape of the mouth, much depends on whether it belongs to a man or a woman. The ideal mouth for a man is broad and square while closed, but round and big when open. The Chinese art of face reading suggests that a man with such a mouth will go far in life and hold an important office in his career. It is said that the first and founding emperor of the Tang dynasty, Tai Zhu, had a mouth so wide and majestic that it could accommodate his own fist with ease. (And my own mouth seems to have the same shape!) A big mouth on a man's face is a very good sign, indicating bravery, ambition and an appetite for life.

However, according to the traditional principles of *Mian Xiang*, a big mouth on a woman could suggest negative qualities. It was believed that a woman with a big mouth would be very talkative and too blunt, both characteristics that Chinese men traditionally dislike. Worst of all, it was thought that she might be clumsy and rather greedy. These generalizations reflect the fact that it was Chinese men who originally composed the basic rules of *Mian Xiang*, and they did not want their womenfolk to be more talented, braver or more generous than they themselves were. The rules were therefore biased to help men choose partners whom they could dominate. Nowadays, however, the more favourable interpretations of a big mouth can be applied to both men and women.

A good mouth should be able to cover the teeth completely when closed. A mouth in which the teeth are visible to a degree even when the lips are drawn together denotes a person who is a troublemaker. People with this type of mouth can be very talkative and have a habit of gossiping about others to such an extent that they often find themselves becoming the target of retaliatory verbal attacks.

In *Mian Xiang* there are many different types of mouth.

TIGER MOUTH

The Tiger Mouth is wide, thick, rosy and symmetrical (*see* fig. 88). Such mouths belong to those who come from a very good family background. They will possess high intelligence and strong perseverance. The Tiger Mouth also signifies wealth and good fortune, and its owner will generally enjoy life. When the teeth are well covered, this denotes great honour and high social standing for the owner. People with this shape of mouth make good partners in both business and sex.

fig. 88

DRAGON MOUTH

The Dragon Mouth is huge and broad, with prominent corners. The lips are full and even (*see* fig. 89). Such a mouth denotes wealth, honour, power, access to good food and a happy life.

fig. 89

MONKEY MOUTH

The Monkey Mouth is broad, thin and curved (*see* fig. 90). Such a mouth denotes a person who has extreme cunning and an opportunistic personality. Those with Monkey Mouths are born diplomats and will do well in business. However, they can sometimes become involved in deceit and fraud. They will often have problems making true friends and sustaining friendships.

fig. 90

COW MOUTH

The Cow Mouth is thick and red but relatively small, with corners that point upwards (*see* fig. 91). It tends to appear huge when the owner laughs. The entire shape is neat and well balanced. Such a shape indicates health, wealth, a happy marriage and an artistic character. The owner will be very popular with the opposite sex and may lead a very romantic life.

fig. 91

PIG MOUTH

The Pig Mouth is small and protruding, with thick lips (*see* fig. 92). This shape denotes a lazy character who indulges in material comforts. The owner tends to be very impatient, cowardly and bad-tempered. People with such mouths may find themselves in trouble because of their careless speech. They will receive little help from close ones and will have to find their way through life on their own.

fig. 92

BIRD MOUTH

The Bird Mouth has lips that are protruding and rather thin (*see* fig. 93). This shape denotes a very garrulous character who may do more talking than is proper. Of course, this will land the owner in a lot of trouble, and might damage his or her life or career.

fig. 93

MOUSE MOUTH

The Mouse Mouth is small with thin lips and corners that point downwards (*see* fig. 94). Such a mouth denotes meanness, narrow-mindedness and an opportunistic attitude. Those with Mouse Mouths are always jealous of the success and good luck of others, although they never strive to achieve anything themselves.

fig. 94

RAM MOUTH

The Ram Mouth is small and thin with the corners pointing upwards (*see* fig. 95). Such a mouth denotes a cautious and conservative person, but one who fortunately has a rather happy and optimistic attitude. Those with Ram Mouths are good at planning, and they can be successful in business and accountancy.

fig. 95

FOX MOUTH

The Fox Mouth is huge and wavy (*see* fig. 96). It denotes a person who is tricky and dishonest, and who has a somewhat lecherous character. Those with Fox Mouths will have problems convincing people of the value of what they have to say, as they keep changing their standpoint all the time. People with this shape of mouth tend to marry many times.

fig. 96

CHERRY MOUTH

The Cherry Mouth is small with a thick lower lip that points upwards at the corners (*see* fig. 97). The owner is inclined to be emotional, gentle and intelligent, and often has artistic talents. People born with this kind of mouth can go far, especially if they properly explore the avenues that can lead to fame and wealth. This shape of mouth is usually found on women, and these women will enjoy happy marriages.

fig. 97

The Teeth

It will come as no surprise that the teeth are also deemed worthy of analysis in the Chinese art of face reading. According to my own research, they reveal quite a lot about their owners. In *Mian Xiang*, the teeth are known as 'the Pillars of the Mouth'. Ideally, the teeth should be long, straight and white; they should be closely set in an orderly manner, neither protruding nor receding. Such teeth signify a long life, good relationships, a stable livelihood, intelligence and a good position in life. It is thought to be very lucky to have 32 or more teeth in the mouth.

General Indications

Good and well-developed teeth are signs of a stable livelihood, access to good food and a happy family life.

- Teeth that are rounded, fit nicely together and are very fresh and white indicate very good fortune. They reveal a harmonious and interesting person who has many gifts and who is artistic, intelligent and well balanced.

- Small teeth that are quite straight and even but with lots of gum showing are an indication that the owner is rather self-centred and lacks consideration towards those around him or her.

- Strong and long teeth promise a long life, but not always an easy one. The owner has to work hard, because nothing will come free of charge.

- Teeth that slant inwards indicate a loner: the owner is someone who prefers to do things in his or her own way and who chooses to be alone.

- The two front teeth in the upper row represent the parents. For men, the left tooth represents the father and the right the mother; for women, it is the other way around. If both teeth are nice and strong, the relationship between the parents has also been very strong and enjoyable. If they grow in different directions, the relationship between the parents has been very poor. It is very important to take good care of your front teeth, as they can even indicate the health of your parents. If the teeth are weak, then your parents may suffer from corresponding bad health.

- Space between the two front teeth indicates waste and excessive generosity. I had a gap like this for many years until I went to a dentist to fix it. Now my life is little bit more comfortable, because I have stopped spending my money thoughtlessly.

The Shape of the Teeth

JADE TEETH

Jade Teeth are white, delicate yet broad, and closely set against each other (*see* fig. 98). They are considered to be lucky because they denote success, wealth and good health.

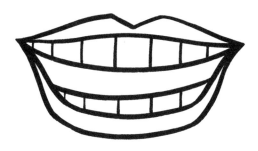

fig. 98

LEAKY TEETH

Leaky Teeth are loosely set, with gaps between them (*see* fig. 99). They indicate instability in finances and relationships. The gaps signify the leakage of money and information.

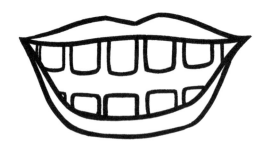

fig. 99

DEVIL'S TEETH

Devil's Teeth are crooked and in great disorder (*see* fig. 100). Such teeth indicate a mean person who is jealous and calculating. People with such teeth are often frustrated in financial and romantic matters, and they can expect little help from friends and family in times of difficulty.

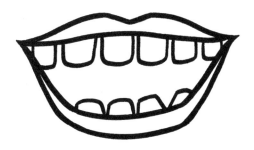

fig. 100

OUTWARDLY POINTING TEETH

Outwardly Pointing Teeth point outwards and away from the centre of the mouth (*see* fig. 101). They denote people who have very outgoing personalities and who may achieve success away from their homelands. People with such teeth are usually self-made and often establish their families far away from the place of their birth. Many successful comedians have Outwardly Pointing Teeth, as they are a sign that the owner is witty and humorous.

fig. 101

DOG TEETH

People with Dog Teeth have two pointed teeth on each side of the upper row (*see* fig. 102). These teeth indicate a person who might bring bad luck to his or her loved ones.

fig. 102

BROAD TEETH

Broad Teeth (*see* fig. 103) symbolize honesty, lots of energy, a good appetite and an outgoing personality. People with such teeth make better friends than those with Leaky Teeth or Devil's Teeth.

fig. 103

Laughter Lines

Laughter lines – called *Fa Ling* in *Mian Xiang* – run from the corners of the nose and down alongside the mouth. They indicate the longevity and achievements of the owner. Ideally, they should be long and curved, as this indicates good health and long life.

These lines are often not very pronounced when people are young, but they usually become clearer when they approach the age of 35 or 40. It is said that it is better if laughter lines are not etched on the face until middle age or later. If they appear earlier, they are considered to be slightly unlucky, although some executives may have such lines in their early thirties.

General Indications

In the Chinese art of face reading there are five basic kinds of laughter lines.

- Laughter lines that are very long, curving down and then out (*see* fig. 104). This is a very good formation, indicating someone who may live for a very long time, maybe even seeing five generations of descendents.

fig. 104

146

- Laughter lines that are long and continue to curve out below the mouth (*see* fig. 105). These mean a long life with much vitality and activity in later years.

fig. 105

- Laughter lines that only reach to the outer corners of the mouth, are curved and are of average length (*see* fig. 106). The owner of these laughter lines will probably have an average lifespan and will enjoy life.

fig. 106

- Laughter lines that are long and curve in below the mouth (*see* fig. 107). These indicate a long life but possible loneliness at the end.

fig. 107

- Laughter lines that curve into the corners of the mouth (*see* fig. 108). These indicate digestive problems in old age.

fig. 108

The Chin

In *Mian Xiang*, the chin is referred to as the 'Earth' region of the face. It is the lowest part of the face and is therefore related to the period of old age. The chin reveals a lot of information about the owner's old age, and especially about the owner's welfare and fortune at the beginning of his or her sixties. This the time when most of us will be thinking about retirement, and also a time when people are concerned about the state of their health.

A good chin signifies a lucky old age with financial security, a good family life and good health. A full, meaty and strong chin usually indicates strength, willpower, sex drive and material comfort. A chin that is weak, thin, short and receding usually indicates an old age spent in financial difficulty, loneliness and poor health. Those with such a chin are advised to marry someone with a stronger chin in order to compensate for this and improve their luck.

The Nine Types of Chin

PROTRUDING CHIN

A chin that protrudes and points upwards towards the forehead (*see* fig. 109) is a clear symbol of power and strength. This is especially true when

fig. 109

the chin not only protrudes, but is also long and broad. People with such chins are born leaders in their fields. They have usually reached the top of their chosen careers by the beginning of their sixties. By the age of retirement, they will find themselves in the most satisfactory part of their lives in terms of power and glory. They are bound to have a relaxed, rewarding and happy old age, no matter what they choose to do. It is also said that people with such chins will have big families with many children and grandchildren.

DOUBLE CHIN

There is a common misconception that a double chin (*see* fig. 110) is simply the result of being overweight. However, in most cases this is not true, for a double chin can be found on people who are not fat at all. A double chin signifies comfort, professional success and a good financial position in old age. It is also a sign of a large appetite for good food and sex.

fig. 110

SQUARE CHIN

A chin that is broad and square (*see* fig. 111) denotes strong determination and great endurance in sexual acts; it is also a sign of wealth and a happy and active old age.

fig. 111

POINTED CHIN

A short and pointed chin (*see* fig. 112) indicates that the owner may experience some weakness as he or she ages. This type of chin can also be a sign that the person will suffer from a sudden disease, be involved in an accident, or go bankrupt. Those with such a chin will have to take extra care as they approach the age of sixty. The best thing for them to do is to get into a partnership with someone who has a strong and broad chin, as then matters will develop much more smoothly. In extreme cases, they might even consider plastic surgery to make the chin a little bigger and broader, as life may start to flow in the right direction after the operation.

fig. 112

RECEDING CHIN

A receding chin (*see* fig. 113) indicates an old age marked by pessimism, a passive attitude towards life, lack of strength and sexual appetite, and problems with finances and relationships. Once again, if those with receding chins choose the right partner, make some preparations, or even consider plastic surgery, life is sure to get back on track during their old age.

fig. 113

ROUND CHIN

A round chin (*see* fig. 114) is a sign of a good appetite for both food and sex. It also indicates a love of luxury and a good financial position in old age.

fig. 114

LONG CHIN

A long chin (*see* fig. 115) denotes business skills, practical qualities and a long life.

fig. 115

DIMPLED CHIN

Dimpled chins (*see* fig. 116) are usually found on people with great artistic talents. A lot of Hollywood stars are blessed with such a chin. However, people with this type of chin can be a little finicky, and they tend to marry more than once. If the chin is also strong and broad, wealth and success in old age are indicated.

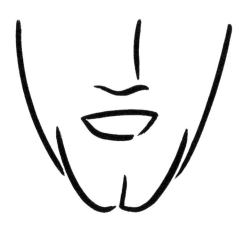

fig. 116

MOUNTED CHIN

This chin is very distinctive and stands out against the nose (*see* fig. 117). People with mounted chins are good at making money and spending it on luxuries. They also have strong sexual drives that may result in more than one marriage.

fig. 117

6

Personal Appearance

Hair, Skin and Forehead Auras

The Hair

ALTHOUGH THE HAIR ON THE HEAD is not strictly a facial feature, *Mian Xiang* nevertheless takes its appearance into account, since hair is associated visually with the face. In fact, the quality of the hair and the beard are both rather important in the Chinese art of face reading. Hair and beards are thought to represent the cosmic energy known as yin – the passive, feminine, receptive energy. In traditional Chinese medicine, the hair and the beard are thought to represent the condition of the blood, the nutrient of life.

General Indications

In the art of Chinese face reading, it is thought to be a sign of good health and vitality when the hair and the beard are shiny and smooth, and neither too coarse nor too abundant. Here are some other general indications.

- If the hair is too thick, the Chinese say that it is draining strength from the body, as the blood is nourishing the hair at the expense of living tissue. However, the hair should not be too thin and delicate either, for this means that the blood is thin and weak.

- If the hair is coarse, it is thought to denote someone who is impulsive, active, aggressive, and usually bad-tempered. A person with coarse hair is an achiever who likes to do things on his or her own. If the hair is extremely coarse, this indicates someone who may be very tempestuous and opinionated, and who can be a powerful opponent to those around him or her.

- Hair that is very thick and bushy or very heavy means a hard life for the owner. If the hair is overabundant, the person is overly emotional and may lack more refined qualities.

- Hair that is soft, bright and shiny indicates a person who can reach a high position and make good money. If the hair is also fine, this is a sign of someone who is sensitive, artistic and creative. However, the owner can also be overly sensitive and rather timid, lacking the kind of drive needed in order to achieve goals. Nonetheless, this is a very intelligent person with a fine character and an even temperament.

- Very thin hair indicates a person who is shrewd but in whom vitality and energy are diminishing; such a person may become old prematurely.

- If the hair is thin and flat, the owner will be vain and love flattery. This person may be very insecure.

- Curly hair shows a person who is intelligent but who can be very fickle at times.

- Very straight hair indicates those who are compassionate but who may lack the drive to get through life.

- In China, balding is considered to be a sign of wealth, and it is also a sign of intellectual growth after the age of 40. It is considered better if the hair merely thins in old age and is not entirely lost._

163

Hair Colour

The hair should preferably be dark and strong in order to show vitality and good health. Hair that goes grey early indicates a very active life ahead. Hair that greys gradually in middle age is an indicator of success and achievement. Hair that is grey in old age is a sign of honour.

Patterns of Hair Growth

- It is thought to be a fortunate sign if the hair does not grow too low behind the ears or around the temples. Nor should the hair invade the plain of the forehead.

- If the hairline starts low in the forehead area, well below the normal position for the hairline, it indicates someone who may be unstable or of low mentality. However, this is a rare sight and should not be confused with a low forehead.

- If the hairline is uneven on a very low forehead, it indicates complexities in the personality.

- If the hairline is low but does not invade the forehead, it is nonetheless still an unfortunate sign. The owner may have a very difficult adolescence, during which there will be a great lack of love and understanding from parents.

- A high hairline indicates a very good relationship with parents.

- If the hairline is very high and at the same time rather square, it can indicate a difficult marriage that might end in divorce.

- Hair that grows to a point in the middle of the forehead, making the hairline look like an 'M', is an indication of charm and flirtatiousness. This kind of hairline is especially fortunate for women, as it reveals a romantic and creative person who is also capable of handling money matters.

- An extremely angular hairline indicates a person with aggressive executive capacities and resourcefulness. This person is strongly focused on carving out a good career, often at the expense of family life.

Beard Patterns

The Chinese strive for balance in most things, not least when it comes to analysing a beard. Allowing the beard to grow is thought to be a demonstration of manhood and power. Beards are also said to have a protective effect for their owners: if misfortune occurs, the beard will be capable of shielding the person by absorbing the shock.

The beard is also said to have something to do with sexuality, and it is thought to be a positive sign for sexual vitality if the beard grows within the area of the philtrum. A beard that is not too coarse or bristly, or too thin or fine, indicates that its owner possesses excellent qualities.

The best kind of beard has a clear pattern of growth, does not reach too high on the cheeks, and has a clear outline. It should also grow evenly, not in whorls or with irregular thickness.

The Skin

Ideally, the skin should smooth, unbroken and seamless. Scars, birthmarks and blemishes are considered unfortunate. If one falls on a Position Point for any given year, it is a warning that extra care and caution are needed at that particular time of life. Moles, on the other hand, may indicate good fortune. However, always remember that healthy moles have a sound colour and are not painful: if they do change colour or become very painful, you should go to a skin-doctor to have them checked.

Moles on the Face

In the Chinese art of face reading, moles indicate a source of strength. It is said that their force is under control when they are hidden from view, whereas the force of an exposed mole is not under control. The strange thing is that if you have a mole somewhere on your face, you will usually have a corresponding mole on your body.

The good or bad fortune indicated by moles on the face varies from position to position, and they may even be both fortunate and unfortunate at the same time.

THE THIRD EYE

– FOREHEAD MOLE

A mole in the middle of the forehead (*see* fig. 118) indicates high intelligence. It is often referred to as the 'Third Eye'. People with such a positive mole will be intelligent, foresighted and very reasonable.

fig. 118

TWO DRAGONS PLAYING WITH A PEARL

– MOLE BETWEEN EYES

This mole is at Position Point 35 between the eyes (*see* fig. 119). This is a very fortunate mole, provided it is light and bright in color. It indicates that the possessor will achieve a high position and may become very worldly and sophisticated.

fig. 119

THE TRAVELLER'S MOLE

– ON OUTER EYEBROW

A mole at the outer tip of the eyebrow (*see* fig. 120) indicates a lot of travel and activity. It also means that the possessor may lack domestic stability.

fig. 120

THE PHILANDERER'S MOLE

– AT OUTER EYE

A mole which is positioned either at the outer tip of the eye or below the outer corner of the eye (*see* fig. 121) is the sign of a flirt or philanderer. It is considered to be attractive, romantic and sexy, but the possessor may be very fickle in love or even adulterous.

fig. 121

THE WEEPING MOLE

– UNDER EYE

The weeping mole is found directly below the middle of the eye (*see* fig. 122). It indicates unhappiness, often because its possessor has problems in love.

fig. 122

THE OBSTINATE MOLE

– ON UPPER CHEEK

A mole on the upper part of the cheek (*see* fig. 123) indicates power and strength, but owners of such moles may be so stubborn that they sometimes forget to be considerate. Consequently, instead of making friends with people around them, they end up making enemies instead.

fig. 123

THE CHARMER'S MOLE

– ON LOWER CHEEK

A mole on the lower part of the cheek (*see* fig. 124) indicates charm, fortune, and luck in marriage. Many portrait painters like to paint a mole in this place to stress the charm and radiance of their subject.

fig. 124

THE GOURMET MOLE

The Gourmet Mole is positioned just above the upper lip (*see* fig. 125), indicating that the owner enjoys gourmet food and the other good things in life. It is definitely a positive mole and is possessed by many of the best chefs in the best restaurants around the world. If you notice that your chef has such mole, you can rest assured that you are in good hands and are eating at the right restaurant. People with this kind of mole are usually very service-oriented and friendly, but they may be overly self-indulgent and difficult to please.

fig. 125

THE FLAMBOYANT MOLE

– ON THE CHIN

A mole at the outer corner of the chin indicates a person who is colourful but who may be a busybody and a rather talkative person (*see* fig. 126).

fig. 126

EAR MOLES

Ear moles (*see* fig. 127) are considered to be fortunate: they promise high achievement, a good position in life, and a good relationship with parents.

- A mole on the upper part of the ear indicates intelligence.

- A mole on the middle part of the ear indicates love and affection for parents.

- A mole on the earlobe indicates wealth and an understanding of business matters.

fig. 127

NOSE MOLES

A mole on the tip of a man's nose (*see* fig. 128) is said to give him a lot of charm and to make him very popular with women. A man with such a mole can have almost any woman he wants.

fig. 128

Moles on the Body

Generally speaking, moles on the body are only considered fortunate if they are covered by clothing or otherwise hidden away from sight. These kinds of mole can often be found on the soles of the feet or behind the ears.

MOLE ON THE THROAT

As we have seen, moles that are considered lucky are usually those which are hidden from view. Therefore, moles on the throat (*see* fig.129) are not thought to be very favourable, as they are usually easy to see. When found on a man, they can indicate feminine traits; when found on a woman, they reveal a certain masculinity. It is said that it is not easy to live with those who have this type of mole: in extreme cases, the presence of such a mole suggests that its owner will have to be especially careful and considerate if his or her marriage is to succeed. People with this type of mole have a tendency to be overly possessive and to cling to their partners, but if they correct this attitude they will enjoy happy relationships, and the mole may even disappear.

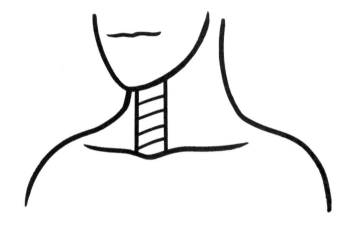

fig. 129

180

MOLE ON THE SHOULDER AREA

A mole in this area (*see* fig.130) belongs to those who will have to work hard to earn a living. From the moment that the mole appears, the affected individual will have to carry big financial burdens.

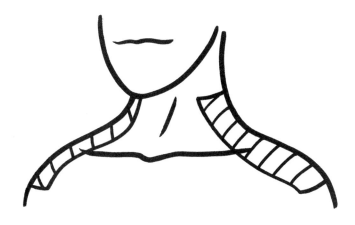

fig. 130

MOLE ON THE COLLARBONE

This is a very favourable spot on which to have a mole (*see* fig.131), as it signifies that the owner is very diplomatic and is well loved and respected by those around him or her. People with this type of mole are good at handling others and always get the help that they need.

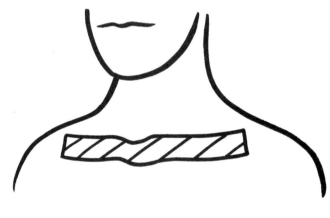

fig. 131

MOLE ON THE UPPER CHEST AREA

This type of mole (*see* fig.132) indicates those possessed of a good heart and great affection for others. People born with such a mole are always kind-hearted and self-sacrificing. They will do whatever is necessary to keep their friends, relatives and those they love happy. Such people make excellent aid-workers.

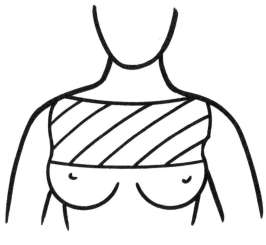

fig. 132

MOLE ON THE BREAST

This is also a very favourable spot for a mole (*see* fig.133), as it indicates that love and children will come easily for the owner. Life is sure to be kind to people with such moles: they will have loving partners and – if they wish – as many children as they want.

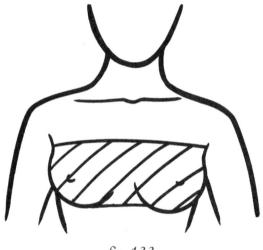

fig. 133

MOLE IN THE ARMPIT

This is another favourable indication. Those who have a mole in their armpit (*see* fig.134) are credible types: they always live up to their promises. (Banks would do well to check their customers for this credit-worthy indication when they are considering loan applications!)

fig. 134

MOLE ON THE STOMACH

This is a very lucky sign which also indicates excellent parenting skills (see fig.135). Those with this type of mole will always love and protect their children, and they will be able to establish a good rapport with them. Also, these people will always be contented with their achievements.

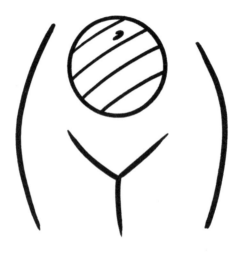

fig. 135

MOLE ON THE LOWER PART OF THE STOMACH

This is a most interesting mole, as it indicates that its owner is a master of the art of lovemaking (see fig.136). However, the owner will have to be careful, as excessive activity in this sphere may eventually lead to problems.

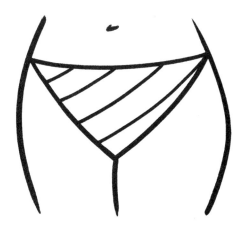

fig. 136

MOLE ON THE BACK OF THE NECK

This is not an especially favourable mole, as it indicates general restlessness and resulting exhaustion. Those with this type of mole would do well to take life easy and get themselves back on an even keel. If they can do this, the mole might even disappear. (*See* fig. 137 for this and all the remaining body moles.)

MOLE ON THE UPPER PART OF THE BACK

This type of mole belongs to people who are very stubborn and who like to run the entire show. Instead of making friends, these people may easily make enemies. It is therefore very important for them to make concerted efforts to be diplomatic and friendly towards others.

MOLE ON THE SIDES OF THE UPPER BACK

This is one of the most favourable positions in Chinese Mole Analysis. A mole in this area indicates a person who is friendly and diplomatic: money will come easily to people with such moles because of these good qualities. This type of mole is generally a sign of a very capable businessperson who will go far in life.

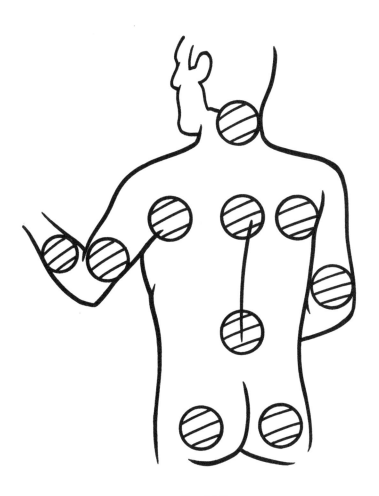

fig. 137

189

MOLE ON THE BACK THAT CORRESPONDS
WITH STOMACH ON OPPOSITE SIDE

This mole is the star of luck and prosperity. It is said that Tang Yuen Zhong, one of the most famous rulers of China, had such a mole on his back. It is a reliable indication of a person who will find it easy to establish his or her reputation, position and financial security. Owners of this type of mole are more or less born with silver spoons in their mouths. (That said, the author of this book has such a mole, but he still has to work hard to make ends meet!)

MOLE ON THE BEHIND

This is a relatively fortunate mole, as it belongs to those who will have lots of luck in love. They will be admired and adored by the people around them. However, they have a tendency to fall in love rather more often than might be considered good for them, which may prove rather strenuous at times!

MOLE ON THE UPPER ARM

This is a very fortunate mole, as it belongs to those who are hardworking and ambitious enough to get things done properly. Many great artists and celebrities have moles on their upper arms.

MOLE ON THE FOREARM

This is a very nice mole to have, as it belongs to those who are practical and reliable. They will always keep their promises and never let anyone down who needs their help. Those with this type of mole can look forward to having many friends, and life will be easy for them.

Freckles

Freckles are considered to be a sign of someone friendly. They also indicate that the person possesses strong sex appeal.

Pimples

It is no small matter for pimples to suddenly appear on the face, as the point at which they crop up can have implications both medically and in terms of a person's destiny. Generally speaking, the Chinese believe that pimples can act as warning signs according to where they appear, so their significance should not be underrated.

Seen from a medical perspective, pimples are a sign of puberty when they appear on the face of a person between the ages of 12 and

19. According to Chinese wisdom, they appear more frequently on boys' faces than on girls', as pimples are signs of abundant energy. Even so, they can be warning signs, as those with abundant energy can be rather impulsive, reckless and rebellious, and they tend to fight with family and friends. Pimples at certain points on the adolescent face might indicate such a potential flare-up, but they should disappear once the young person calms down.

Here is a list of some of the ways in which pimples can act as warning signs, whatever the age of the person affected by them.

- A pimple that suddenly appears on the laughter lines around the mouth (*see* fig.138) indicates that the owner

fig. 138

has a very stressed relationship with his or her parents or peers. Such people may well be on a collision course with their bosses, and it is very important for them to cool down. When the pimple starts to disappear, it is a sign that balance is returning.

- A pimple that suddenly appears on one of the cheekbones (*see* fig.139) indicates that the person's plans are heading in the wrong direction and that he or she will have to make certain adjustments to get by. Once again, when the pimple starts to disappear, this means that things are returning to normal again.

fig. 139

- A pimple on the forehead (*see* fig.140) indicates relationship difficulties between the person and his or her parents. It would be wise for this person to pay more attention to his or her parents: when the relationship is mended, the pimple will disappear.

fig. 140

- A pimple or two near the eyes (*see* fig.141) indicates someone who may have quarrelled with his or her partner or loved ones. It is vital to make up, because then peace and harmony will be restored to the person's life.

fig. 141

- A pimple on the nose (*see* fig. 142) is a sign of a bad digestion. It is important to have the right meals at the right times, so this person should try to sort out his or her diet. The pimple will disappear when things are back on track.

fig. 142

- A woman who suddenly gets a pimple between the nose and the upper lip (*see* fig.143) should be aware that this can be a sign that something is wrong with her reproductive system. She would be wise to go to a doctor for a check-up.

fig. 143

Luckily, pimples are only a temporary phenomenon: they will disappear as soon as health and vitality are restored. They are nothing to worry about, although preventative measures can be taken to guard against them appearing.

The Forehead Aura

In *Mian Xiang*, the aura radiated by the forehead plays a vital role. Those with a lot of experience in face reading can actually detect the colours on a person's forehead and predict what is going to happen to him or her at a later stage. As long as the forehead's aura is an agreeable and appropriate colour, everything is in balance. However, should negative colours appear, action may need to be taken.

Everyone will have his or her own special charismatic colour. I will share with you the secrets of ten different hues: these are yellow, violet, red, green, white, burning red, black, oiliness, dustiness and darkness.

YELLOW

This shade of yellow is the same colour as sweetcorn. It is a good colour, indicating that money may come in, that there will be good exam results, or that promotion could be on its way. In other words, it is a very favourable colour.

VIOLET

This shade of violet is like refracted sunshine, in which the violet colour is very apparent. This colour means the possibility of winning prizes; alternatively, an unexpected sum of money could arrive, or there could be a sudden favourable change in employment coming along.

RED

This shade of red is the colour of a cherry, fresh and attractive. It is a very good colour, meaning that a wedding may take place very soon, or that a new baby will be born into the family. It is also a sign of strong financial resources.

GREEN

This shade of green is the colour of a fresh cucumber. It means that the person is tired and full of worries. It can also indicate someone who has consumed too much alcohol or is having too much sex.

WHITE

White, the shade of new-fallen snow, is a very unlucky colour, denoting someone who is experiencing health problems. It would be wise for this person to see the doctor for a check-up.

BURNING RED

Deep red, the colour of a burning fire or of meat, is another unfavourable colour. It warns of accidents and fire, the possible misuse of weapons, or even impending legal trials.

BLACK

An unhygienic and dirty black that looks like collected grime is a negative colour, because it warns of the death of someone close.

OILINESS

Oiliness, like the colour of an oil stain, is an aura colour which is seen on people whose close friends may be making trouble for them, or on people who feel as if they are stagnating.

DUSTINESS

An aura that appears to be dusty, as though the owner had been through a sandstorm, indicates someone who is tired and exhausted. People with dusty-looking auras may have travelled far and wide without getting any positive results. They need to take some rest.

DARKNESS

The appearance of a darkness similar to the colour of the sky before rainfall is a warning that something sad is about to happen. People with this type of aura need to take things easy until the situation improves.

7

Mastering the Physical Languages

Face Language and Body Language

OUR FACE AND BODY LANGUAGE can communicate a great deal about us, above and beyond the way we actually talk. The way we humans express ourselves may have undergone dramatic changes through the processes of evolution and civilization, but our faces, arms, fingers and legs remain essential elements in the process of communication.

Face Language

As we saw in the introduction, the basic elements of face language apply more or less the world over. Here are some guidelines to enable you to distinguish between heartfelt emotion and feigned feelings.

HAPPINESS

A truly happy message is best expressed by a contented smile (*see* fig. 144). The lower part of the eyelid is usually slightly raised, and small

fig. 144

wrinkles may appear under the eyes. The mouth widens where the corners of the mouth point upwards. The lips are parted just enough to show the upper row of teeth. The laughter lines are emphasized. The cheeks are raised in a gesture that makes the eyes appear smaller.

SADNESS

A sad message will be expressed by a lowering of the corners of the mouth (*see* fig. 145). The lips may be trembling as grieving or crying commences. The eyebrows will be pointing downwards at the outer corners. A lot of wrinkles may appear on the forehead.

fig. 145

SURPRISE

Genuine surprise is expressed by raising the brow and the eyebrows (*see* fig. 146). The gaze will be magnified, and more of the eyes' whites will appear than usual. The jaw drops, and the mouth opens.

fig. 146

FEAR

Fear is expressed by raising the eyebrows and pulling them together (*see* fig. 147). Wrinkles will appear. The upper eyelids will be raised in order to show the whites of both eyes. The lips will be tightened and pulled together around an open mouth.

fig. 147

ANGER

The muscles around the eyebrows express anger (*see* fig. 148). They are pressed downwards and inwards, so that vertical wrinkles appear between the eyes. The stare is cold and harsh. The lips are tightened, and the corners of the mouth point downwards. The nostrils tend to flare more than usual on an angry face.

fig. 148

DISGUST

Disgust is expressed by raising the eyelids and showing the wrinkles between the eyes (*see* fig. 149). Wrinkles on the nose will appear, and the cheeks will be raised. The upper lip or both lips may also be slightly raised.

fig. 149

Body Language

Psychologists in the West have much in common with Chinese fortune-tellers, as both set great store by body language, believing that it can reveal much about the mental state of a person.

I have come to the following conclusions on body language, which I would like to share with my readers.

- People who are trying to stress something that they know a lot about will stroke one of their thumbs against an index finger (*see* fig. 150).

fig. 150

- People who wave their fists about are trying to emphasize their views (*see* fig. 151).

fig. 151

- A person who bends his or her fingers inwards while talking is trying to establish some semblance of authority (*see* fig. 152).

fig. 152

- Anyone who points at someone else with the index finger is making an unfriendly gesture and means to attack that particular person (*see* fig. 153).

fig. 153

- A person who sits with crossed hands is displaying their disagreement with something (*see* fig. 154).

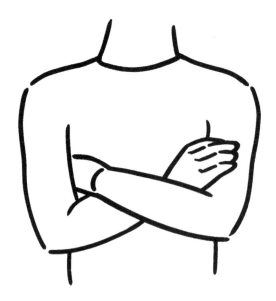

fig. 154

- Someone who does not look you in the eyes when talking to you is either very tired or trying to hide something from you.

- Someone who closes his or her eyes when talking to you has submitted to you totally.

- People who walk almost as if they were on tiptoe are usually pessimistic and shy types.

- Those who walk with their feet pointing outwards are full of self-confidence and are true optimists.

- To show interest, a person will raise the eyebrows, cheeks and lips slightly; he or she may also lean forwards a little bit to emphasize this display of interest.

- It is a good sign if a person sits with his or her chest puffed out, as it signifies lots of energy, good health and self-confidence.

- People who touch their ears all the time like to quarrel, both with words and with fists.

- Somebody who touches his or her nose all the time is not sexually satisfied. Furthermore, such people like to run the show and can be very stubborn and selfish.

In addition to the ways in which people present themselves through their body language, I have observed some other tell-tale signs.

- Those who brag all the time are actually uncertain about themselves.

- Someone who displays arrogance when he or she has met with success will not be a good co-worker.

- Someone who talks about his or her weaknesses all the time is not altogether honest. This person may be difficult to understand and could be very intolerant at times.

- People who choose their words very carefully, yet are willing to make a point when it really matters, are reliable and trustworthy.

- A person who really knows how to use his or her time properly is both wise and effective.

Signs of Flirting

I suspect that most people will use similar body language and follow a similar strategy for flirting as that which I have described in the imaginary scenario below.

John enters a night club and pauses just inside the door. He looks around with his thumbs hitched in the waist of his jeans and his hands hanging loose – a gesture that most men will recognize. John's fingers are pointing towards his crotch, though this is not done in a direct way. Without knowing it, he is already signalling to all the unattached women present that he is looking for a partner. As he stands there, he tries to adjust his senses to the noise and the rather subdued lighting. Then he spies an empty table and makes for it. John sits down with one of his legs crossed slightly over the other so that the ankle rests on the knee. He orders a drink and keeps looking around. He is not quite aware of it yet, but he is already being watched himself, and his every move reveals something about him.

Not far away from John, a group of women sits chatting. They seem to be very wrapped up in each other's conversation, but in reality they are barely listening to each other. As they talk, they keep glancing towards the boys around the club. The women are picking out who they will respond to if asked to dance. One of them, Marie, is really interested in John and keeps glancing in his direction. She may glance coyly at him over a raised shoulder, just long enough to send out interested signals: in body language, a woman's shoulders often correspond with her breasts.

She may also shake her head and throw her hair back from her face in order to expose her face for his admiration. John catches her gaze and keeps on looking at her even after she has looked away. He seems to be very interested as well, but what move should he make?

Once he has realized that Marie keeps looking at him, he starts to look back at her even more frequently. The final moment comes when their eyes meet and their gaze locks. If John can capture this important moment and manage a slight, friendly and warm smile, much will be achieved. Marie may return his smile. Then John will nod perceptibly towards the dance floor. Marie nods back in agreement, perhaps blushing slightly, even though she does not feel especially awkward or embarrassed. John gets up, goes over and asks her to dance. They move on to the dance floor. Without using more than a couple of words, he has surmounted the biggest barrier in human communication. However, the battle is not yet won: there are numerous pitfalls still to avoid.

John and Marie will not have much opportunity to talk, as the music is loud. However, during the dance, they are close enough to find out whether the other is taller or shorter, thinner or fatter, and whether their breath, body odour and voice are desirable.

John and Marie will assess each other indirectly to decide whether the other gives the requisite amount and kind of eye contact, and to determine what is being communicated by facial expression, body posture, gesture and a whole number of other nonverbal behaviours. If things are going well, Marie may abandon her friends and sit down with John between dances. But how can John know that Marie fancies him and is not just passing the time until someone better comes along? What kinds of signals will she give?

If John looks into Marie's eyes, he may notice that her pupils are dilated. This is not an indication that she is drugged or drunk, but rather that she is very interested in John. (Likewise, his interest in her will register in his own eyes.) Marie's skin may even have a reddish tone to it, even though she is not blushing or feeling especially shy. This is a very favourable sign and shows that she is extremely interested in John.

Now we can leave John and Marie in the certainty that, even though they have not had a chance to talk properly, their bodies have already spoken and expressed their interest in each other. And if they want to know even more about each other without asking directly, they can always apply the principles of *Mian Xiang* to read the subtleties of each other's faces.

Appendix

Face Reading and the Animal Kingdom

THE CHINESE HAVE PRACTISED face reading for thousands of years. However, they believe that it is not only possible to create a thorough analysis for humans, but that even animals' forms and behaviour can be interpreted, enabling us to understand them properly.

Birds, cats, dogs, horses and even crickets can be analysed. When I was a child, I used to collect crickets for fighting. And, of course, noisy crickets with big heads, strong necks, sharp claws, compact stomachs and long, sensitive horns always made the best fighters.

I had also a cat when I was a boy. I was told that cats with very relaxed feet are lazy. Cats with very pointed noses and mouths will be fond of stealing food to eat. A cat with a coloured tongue likes to catch chickens, whereas a cat with vertical patterns on its forehead will prefer to catch mice. A cat with a long tail is an agile animal that can leap high and low. A cat with horizontal lines near the jaws is a hard worker and very effective weapon against rats and mice. Vermin will also be kept at bay by a cat with oily, feline-smelling feet. Cats born during summer will be afraid of the cold and prefer to stay near the fireplace during winter. If the litter is particularly small the kittens will grow into strong and very good cats, as their mother will be able to devote more time to each of them than if there were many.

A good hunting dog has certain distinguishable features. A dog with a big head, pointed mouth, strong chest, slim stomach and strong feet is a good hunting animal. Friendly, cute dogs will be able to touch their masters' hearts, and stay comfortably by the fire at home, where their masters treat them like princes and princesses.

It is quite clear that the face plays an important role in our lives whether we are human or animal. There may even be some crossover, as a feline or canine appearance will certainly influence a human's destiny at different levels. A person's features may actually resemble those of a particular animal, and this will provide clues about that individual's personality. For example, a person who looks a bit like a monkey might have the characteristics of a monkey and be restless and fickle. Somebody who looks like a tiger could be tough and brave. A person who looks like a dog may act like a dog, and be always on guard against trouble and loyal to his or her friends and superiors.

As a general principle, people who resemble one of the twelve animal signs of the Chinese horoscope may share the qualities associated with those signs, which include the rat, ox, tiger, rabbit, dragon, snake, horse, goat, monkey, rooster, dog and pig. For more information about the qualities of the signs, see my annual series of Chinese horoscope books.

Author's Note

I HOPE THAT YOU HAVE ENJOYED sharing my knowledge in this book, and that the information in it will enable you to read the faces of your family, friends and colleagues with ease.

With my expertise in face reading, Chinese horoscopes, the *I Ching* and *feng shui*, I pride myself on being the best and most famous Chinese fortune-teller and astrologer in the world. I am constantly improving my knowledge, and am presently studying the relationships between human genetics and astrology. I can give advice in 7 different languages about many things, including career, love, health and other matters. If you would like to contact me, I can be reached by telephone, fax or E-mail. My address details are as follows:

Henning Hai Lee Yang
Brugaten 1
0189 Oslo
Norway

Tel. (+47) 22 177250
Fax (+47) 22 170542

E-mail : HYPERLINK mailto:yangz@yangz.com
yangz@yangz.com
Http://www.yangz.com   Http://www.wap.com

Index